You Don't Look Like A Minister But You Sure Do Sing Like One

36 Humorous Stories On Church Life

Paul A. Corcoran

CSS Publishing Co., Inc.
Lima, Ohio

YOU DON'T LOOK LIKE A MINISTER

Copyright © 1988 by
CSS Publishing Company, Inc.
Lima, Ohio

All rights reserved. No part of this publication may be reproduced in any manner whatsoever without the prior permission of the publisher, except in the case of brief quotations embodied in critical articles and reviews. Inquiries should be addressed to: Permissions, CSS Publishing Company, Inc., P.O. Box 4503, Lima, Ohio 45802-4503.

This book was originally published under the title "Don't Wash Your Antependia."

Library of Congress Cataloging-in-Publication Data

Corcoran, Paul A., 1923-
　　Don't wash your antependia and other looney tunes from the wonderful world of church.

　　1. Church — Anecdotes, facetiae, satire, etc.   I. Title.
PN6231.C35C6　　1988　　　　　250'.207　　　　　87-34204
ISBN 1-55673-035-7

8820 / ISBN 1-55673-035-7　　　　　　　　　　PRINTED IN U.S.A.

Acknowledgments

The following articles are reprinted from *The Presbyterian Outlook*, 512 E. Main Street, Richmond, Virginia, with the permission of the publisher:

"Don't Wash Your Antependia," "A Bit of Chic," "Credit Card Religion," "No Reverends, Please," "Phenomenoniacs," "Whichever Way You Hang It," "Doubt and Out," "The Clergy Nightmare," "Ho-Ha-88," "Pew Pencils," "Boggles and Bagels," "Shortspeak," "Pewology," "The Van Advantage," " 'Do You Speak . . .?' ", "Spider, Spider, On the Mike," "You Are What You Eat," "Let Us Pray," "Thus May Become So," "Proverbs a la Carte," "Up, Up, A Little Bit Higher," "Preacher in the Pew," "Holy Ingenuity," "The More Things Change,""I'd Like to Know," "The Cookie Monster," "The Future Is in the Bag."

"Let Us Pray" appeared in *Theology Today*, P.O. Box 29, Princeton, New Jersey, and is reprinted with their permission.

Preface

Things don't always have to mean something. What does a warm breeze mean? It's just nice, and that's enough. What does the smell of wet lilacs mean? Or the feel of velvet? Or the sound of a door closing with a solid "thunk"? Or a rhyme? Or a sunny park bench? They're just nice, and the dolt who comes along and interprets them only spoils them for us.

As the author of this collection, I claim the right to insist that you not put these essays under any undue strain to mean something. The fact that they come out of the world of church doesn't imply that they are pregnant with theology or morality. They aren't meant to make any intellectual or ethical demands on you. If a piece gives you a sudden jag in the funny nerve, that's meaning enough. If something rewards you with an outright laugh, it's a bonus. If there should be a subtle point here and there, just take it for what it's worth and don't wonder about hidden agendas. There aren't any, except perhaps to share some moments of fun over things we've both run into in the wonderful world of church.

I am grateful to Mike Sherer and C.S.S. for publishing this second collection of my modest writings. Neither of us expects this book to usher in the Kingdom, nor even save the whales, but I hope it will prove as profitable to the publisher as it is satisfying to me. Your buying this copy has helped in both ways.

For the hard work of editing, typing, correcting, and retyping the manuscript, which she managed in between housekeeping, cooking, baking, and being a deacon and choir member in the church, I am unspeakably grateful to my wife Leila. Every minister should have one wife who is a good secretary.

> Paul A. Corcoran
> Lansdale, Pa.
> October 24, 1987

Table of Contents

Acknowledgments 3
Preface 5
Don't Wash Your Antependia 8
A Bit of Chic 10
Credit Card Religion 12
No Reverends, Please 14
Phenomenoniacs 16
Whichever Way You Hang It 18
B. S. 20
Doubt and Out 22
The Clergy Nightmare 24
Ho-Ha-88 26
Pew Pencils 29
Boggles and Bagels 31
Shortspeak 33
Pewology 35
The Van Advantage 37
"Do You Speak . . .?" 40
Spider, Spider, on the Mike 42
Gift Horses 44
You Are What You Eat 46
Burnout 48
Let Us Pray 50
Thus May Become So 52
Your Own Personal Star 54
Proverbs a la Carte 56

Up, Up, A Little Bit Higher	59
Senior Citizen Discount	61
The Nicest Words	63
Preacher in the Pew	66
Holy Ingenuity	68
Balconies	71
Prayerfully Consider	73
The More Things Change	75
I'd Like to Know	77
The Cookie Monster	79
Start Praying	81
The Future Is in the Bag	83

Don't Wash Your Antependia

Some people within the church have been saying that we ought to learn to call things by their proper ecclesiastical names. Our elders had a meeting about it and they all agreed, only nobody could think of any examples. So we called a recess and sent one of them out for an encyclopedia and two more for doughnuts.

Starting under "A" in the encyclopedia, we discovered that we should be calling the pulpit scarves "antependia," *ante* for "in front of," and *pendium* for "something that hangs." An antependium is something that "hangs in front of the pulpit." A preacher is something that hangs on the back of the pulpit and sometimes leans on top of it. One elder, who attended an Episcopal kindergarten when he was young and never got over it, boasted that he even knew what the colors of the antependia mean. "White is for weddings," he said, "black is for funerals, red is for Christmas, purple means Lent, and green means summertime." I recalled that a church we once attended didn't have a purple one but had a lavender one, which means you should never wash your antependia.

You may already know about antependia, but maybe you are — as we were — one of the many churches that have an overflow section and don't know a better name for it. It is really called the "transcept," from *trans* meaning "across" and *septum* meaning "enclosure." The transcept is the enclosure across from something. In our case it's across from the choir. So our overflow is really our transcept. I like that better, because "overflow" always sounded like some kind of plumbing problem.

Before you start calling it a transcept, however, you have to have one on the other side. Transcepts come in pairs, every south having a north, and every north a south, just like in Dakotas and Carolinas. What's over there on our north side is the choir loft. You can call it a transcept if you wish, but it's really a choir loft, and you can't go in there unless you're willing to sing and wear a green robe. A mere transcept is open to anybody who can stay awake during the sermon.

There is an ecclesiastical place for the choir. It's called, with divine logic, the "choir," and it's located along both sides of the chancel, in back of the pulpit. We don't have a choir because we don't have a chancel. We don't even have an in-back-of-the-pulpit. I don't mean to say that we haven't a choir. We have a very good one. We just don't have a "choir" for them to sit in, only a choir loft which really ought to be a transcept.

Now, if we had a chancel, and I'm not suggesting we go out and get one, not even a used one — but if we did, we could have a "choir." We could also have our own "presbytery," which isn't what it sounds like to Presbyterians, but is a sort of stall located between the pulpit and the chancel where the clergy sit so they won't have to sit with the choir in the "choir," and where they can keep their thermos of coffee. Every ecclesiastically correct church should have one. People who do have one say that it's very reassuring to enter the church and see that

the preacher is in his presbytery,
all's right with the world.

You can see that our elders don't have an easy aisle to walk concerning this matter of ecclesioterminology. They managed to get straight about antependia, but they still have a south transcept without a north one, a choir that doesn't have a "choir" to sit in, and no presbytery except the Presbyterian kind that holds meetings and levies per capita taxes. On top of that, the doughnuts were all gone.

So they did what elders do best: they tabled the matter and adjourned with prayer. Next month is always a better time to figure things out.

A Bit of Chic

A friend of mine, who is the chaplain at one of those exclusive prep schools, says that he knows he has his work cut out for him when the students start asking to be baptized in Perrier water. I know how he feels. I once had a family join the church and then ask if they could have their communion bread toasted.

Well, why not? A touch of class is good for anybody. You know, that bread Jesus used wasn't just little cubes of Grandpa Stroehman's Enriched White. And the wine? Well, let's put it this way: when he supplied the wine for the wedding party at Cana, the guests thought the host had brought out his best private stock. Christian Brothers Sauvignon, I imagine. It certainly wasn't Mogen David Ceremonial. Jesus didn't mind a few nice touches here and there. Gloom is for Satan, and serves him right.

So I don't mind people making requests for something special. It's fine that they want to drag the church out of Dullsville. For too long we have had the notion that drabness is next to godliness, and blessed are the bored for they shall inherit the earth. If they do, they can keep it. God and I will be off to somewhere more interesting.

So I say "good," if some of my fellow clergy have taken to wearing shirts of mint green, or royal blue, or even protestant pink, with their clerical collar. No problem. The collar is still there to show their holiness and keep them safe from muggers and traffic tickets, but meanwhile they make life a bit more colorful for us all. And what's wrong with preaching in an Arnold Palmer blazer? A person can be humble and stylish at the same time, you know.

Dressing up religion isn't a bad idea. A little touch of this, a little bit of that. Shows you know how to do it right. If the Lord loves a cheerful giver, he certainly appreciates one with a bit of chic. He who made the caviar, and gave mankind wool worsted, and put the Rolls next to the Royce, surely doesn't mind when people act like going to church is one of the class things to do.

Variety, you know, is the spice of life, and I really don't think the Lord takes away points when we try to put a little of it into the church. In fact, I think it is rather theological. "Behold the birds of the air . . . " "Behold the lilies of the field . . ." Behold the snowflake (no two alike). God invented variety. As one of my black friends says, "Paul, if the Lord had wanted the world to be dismal, he would have made everybody un-colored like you."

So, lately, I have been looking around for ways to add a touch of class to our church. We could put an atrium in the lobby, or a salad bar. How about gold cushions on the pews? Air-conditioning with scented air? Box seats for VIPs and double-tithers. Red carpet all the way out the front walk? People would notice.

All nice, but I think the answer is much easier. All we have to do to add some class to our church is get you to come around more often, because you're some of the classiest people I know.

Credit Card Religion

It's just a flat little bit of plastic worth maybe two cents, small enough to hold in the palm of your hand. It's also one of the most powerful bits of stuff in the world. Like plutonium, a little bit of it can produce huge results. It's your credit card, and it can get you the world without a nickel in your pocket: clothes, food, entertainment, anything your heart desires. It can also get you a peck of trouble around the first of the month.

The one place where your credit card will get you absolutely nothing is in church. You may as well leave home without it if that's where you're headed. The church is still on a cash-and-carry basis.

Maybe it's time to change all that and get the church into the world of the 80s. I don't mean just letting you use your credit card to charge your offering when you forget to bring cash. Not that we would object to the healthy tithe you would charge to your VISA card, but that's barely scratching the surface of the possibilities. All sorts of new worlds could open up, once we got used to a pray now, pay later system.

You could charge sins, for instance, living it up all month long and consolidating your repentance into one convenient prayer meeting at the end of the month. We could even establish a rotating line of credit that would allow you to repent as little as ten minutes each month against any outstanding balance of sins. Only a small handling charge on the unrepented balance would be assessed. We can even arrange credit insurance, so that if anything should happen to you while there were outstanding sins, your heirs would not be saddled with the burden. The sins of the fathers don't really need to be visited upon the sons unto the third and fourth generation.

You should be able to charge church attendance too. After all, you're a very busy person, as we all know (your wife keeps telling us). Sometimes it just isn't possible for you to find time for church. Not to worry, just charge it. We'll have two convenient plans for you to choose from. Plan A is for anyone who has been a paid-up church member for two years. It lets you charge attendance three weeks in a row, as long as you show up for communion each month. Just submit a letter from the boss saying that you do indeed have to work hard all week and need Saturday and Sunday to unwind.

Plan B, our Golden Halo Plan, is for anyone who has been a member for five years. We issue you a personal card embossed with a golden halo which allows you up to twenty-six weeks of absence, as long as you make it on Christmas and Easter. It also admits you to the reserved pews in the farthest back of the church and gives you a doodle pad and pencil with your initials printed on them — also in gold. To qualify, just send next year's offerings in advance, accompanied by an affidavit from at least two impartial neighbors verifying that you regularly are observed worshiping God in your own way at home, and that you never say anything but good about your minister. We'll get your Golden Halo card on its way to you without delay.

Credit card religion could be the main-line church's answer to television evangelism and the Moral Majority. It won't let you be two places at the same time, but it's the next thing to it. You can be home in bed without feeling guilty about not being in church, because you know it's on your charge, and you will pay your bill when the time comes.

That time is called Judgment Day, but why worry about that now? The world may not last that long, anyway.

No Reverends, Please

Would you like to be smarter than your television set? Be ahead of your newspaper? Be right about something most people get wrong? To climb this peak and look down on the uninformed world, all you need do is learn the proper use of "Reverend."

I discovered this secret when Jesse Jackson became a candidate for the Democratic nomination and the news media found themselves having to take a clergyman more seriously than they are accustomed to doing. From the start they didn't know what to call him, except "Reverend." So, they began to "Reverend" him all over the place. It was "Reverend Jackson" this, and "Reverend Jackson" that, and "Reverend Jackson spoke today to the Future Beekeepers of America."

These weren't amateurs doing this. I'm talking Phil Donahue. I'm talking the *Today Show*. I'm talking network anchors who make ten times your salary just for reading the news. Dictionaries don't seem to be one of their tools of the trade. "It shall not be so among you" — to quote the Bible. "You shall know the truth, and the truth shall make you free."

That liberating truth is that "Reverend" is not a title; it's not even a noun. Webster's Seventh New Collegiate says that it is an honorific, which is a kind of gratuitous adjective applied to a person because of the office that person holds. For instance, "Honorable" is the honorific for a judge or a congressman. "Venerable" is the honorific for leaders in some of the older order churches. And "Reverend" is the honorific for a clergyman.

So, if you see Jesse Jackson coming down the street, you don't say to him, "Hello there, Reverend," unless you are also willing to say to your congressman, "Hello there, Honorable."

If you interviewed him, you wouldn't address him as "Reverend Jackson," unless you would also address Judge Doe as "Honorable Doe." What's right for one honorific is just as right for another, as Funk once said to Wagnall.

The rule is that an honorific is always preceded by "the" and always used with the person's full name. It's always "the Reverend Jesse Jackson," or at least "the Rev. Mr. Jackson." Otherwise, just "Mr. Jackson" is fine, or even just "Jesse," if you know him well enough; in which case could you also please get me his autograph? Get Judge Doe's too, if you can. Who knows when it might come in handy? But please, never "Reverend Jackson." That's worse than calling him a Republican.

Being the Christians we are, what should matter most is what the Lord calls us. Clergymen and laymen alike, he calls us all sinners. From our point of view that may not be a very terrific honorific, but it is also not a very specific honorific. I mean, when a preacher says that we are all sinners, he means everyone in the congregation, but never anyone in particular.

When all is said and done (which could be any day now, what with all the megatonnage of nuclear bombs aimed and ready), honorifics, titles, ranks, degrees, and anything else attached to our names won't mean much. The only thing that will matter is whether they have your name spelled right on that roll that's called up yonder.

It's C-O-R-C-O-R-A-N, Lord. You have that? The Reverend Paul A.

Phenomenoniacs

There are some of us that things just happen to. We're like cartoonist Al Capp's little friend Joe Btfskt, who always walked around with a miniature thunderstorm going on over his head. Don't get too close, unless you are used to strange things, or are one of us yourself.

What kind of strange things, you ask? Well, I was walking past a telephone booth one day, not another soul in sight, and the phone began to ring. I answered it; no one was there! That kind of strange thing.

Or this: I went up to a house one day, and on the door there was this sign, "This house guarded by an attack cat." I knocked on the door, and a cat came around the corner of the house and attacked me!

Or this: One day I has pulling into my driveway, and when I pushed the button on the automatic garage door opener, the door didn't open but the doorbell rang, and my wife came out just in time to see me drive through the garage door.

Or this: My dentist has Muzak playing in his office. It's supposed to keep your mind off the drill. I was sitting there listening and I said, "Nice music." He looked at me strangely and said, "I don't have it on today." It was coming out of the fillings in my teeth! I clamped down and it changed stations!

Such is life for us phenomenoniacs. Is it any wonder we have a shifty look to us? It comes from always watching for the next thing to happen. It's like being the target for all million-to-one shots, like having your own Murphy's Law — "If it's weird, it will happen — to you."

Noting all these phenomena, and being personally of the biblical persuasion, I thought one day that I ought to find something in the Scriptures that speaks to us, something to say, "Take heart, you're not the only ones." Maybe some of the early fathers had some random phantoms of their own; it would help us to know. I must report that so far the gleanings are slim. I did find Moses, of course, turning aside to see a bush that was burning, but not burning up. That's sort of like answering a phone booth. And there was Elijah's ax that fell into the river and floated instead of sinking from sight. The prophet never did figure out how to get rid of that ax. He was like the Australian who went crazy trying to throw away an old boomerang. Aside from these two, though, I haven't run across much to reassure us marchers to the beat of a different drummer.

Except that I did find us a patron saint. Let me introduce Asaph, hero of the fiftieth Psalm and one-time choir director in the Temple. Asaph was going over his notes one day before choir practice when out of the clear blue a huge voice boomed down from the high rafters of the Temple: "ASAPH, I WILL ACCEPT NO BULL FROM YOUR HOUSE!" (Honest, it's in Psalm 50.) Asaph looked up startled, scratched his head, and said, "Now what the heck was that all about?" Welcome to the club, Asaph. When the Lord sends you messages like that you know you're on a different wave length than other people.

Of course, isn't that what it's all about, this Christianity? I don't mean weird, I mean hearing a different message than a lot of the world hears. It is kind of a strange message, too; "Sacrifice is better than gain." . . . "The servant shall be greatest of all." . . . "Believe what is not seen." . . . "Seek first the Kingdom of Heaven," when nobody has ever seen the Kingdom of Heaven. Strange words. Strange ideas. Strange way to believe. It makes you, as Peter said, "God's peculiar people." God's "phenomenoniacs."

I'll settle for that, and a new garage door.

Whichever Way You Hang It

A long time ago, I learned that in the Northern Hemisphere, when water goes down a drain it swirls in a counterclockwise direction; men put on their trousers left leg first; and people always eat pie from the point inward. Those are just facts of life up here above the equator. Down-under it's just the opposite. It all has to do with the fact that the North Pole is up there in the Arctic, and the South Pole is down in the Antarctic. It's like the sun always rising in the east and setting in the west, people always sitting in certain pews, and if you're lost in the woods, just keep going north and eventually you'll run into a boy scout or an interstate highway. They're just some of the blessed certainties that keep us sane. "Always" is a very reassuring word.

Well, you can stop saying "always," my friend, because things are in for a change. I'm sorry that I read about him, but there's a geologist out in Minnesota who says there is going to be a polar flip-flop someday. In fact, he says, we're about 500,000 years overdue. What he means by a polar flip-flop is just what you think he means. Every so often the earth's north-south magnetic field just turns itself right around. The South Pole goes north while the North Pole goes south. And it's going to happen again. I mean soon, like within the next 2,000 years — so hold off on buying that ticket for a South Seas cruise. You might be running into some icebergs out there around Pago Pago.

Maybe we'd also better hold up on MX missiles and Star Wars systems till we see what effect this flip-flop is going to have on electronic guidance systems. Right now they're built on the assumption that the water will go down counterclockwise. But what if it reverses? All those little gyros in those little warheads would start spinning the other way and we could end up bombing ourselves, which would be pretty embarrassing. We can accept being disintegrated by some missile from the evil empire, but how do you explain to your kids that it was a made-in-America model that got them? And that it was because the water in the toilet started going clockwise?

Of course, any announcement that comes toward the end of one of those long Minnesota winters has to seem a little suspicious. A person gets tired of watching *Love Boat* and reading Norman Vincent Peale and begins to look around for some way to stir up some excitement. That's especially true for a geologist who has to make his living digging up rocks. So he invents a theory — and people start sending him mail.

> *Dear Dr. _____,*
> *If you weren't one of those atheistic materialists, you would know that what you've discovered is the approach of the Day of Judgment, which the Lord prophesied to visit punishment on non-believers and all those people who belong to those Commie-loving liberalist churches. Repent before it's too late, or else you deserve your fate.*
> *Yours in Christian love,*

> *Dear Professor,*
> *Enclosed please find a contract for your endorsement of our brand of gym shoes. We think a man of your obvious caliber can sell a lot of our newest model, the heel-toe-reversible. Just sign both copies and return them to our head office. We will pay you the minute the flip-flop happens, provided the check doesn't end up in Sydney, Australia.*
> *Yours for Bigger Bucks,*

Probably what the church ought to do is get busy writing a job description for a Flip-Flop Action Enabler, someone to go around and help churches interface with the potentials of reversal and resonate to the felt needs of those who can't cope. It's the least we can do.

The most we can do is get a new church seal, one that looks the same whichever way you hang it.

B. S.

There was a time when "b.s." meant something else, but nowadays it's the initials of a sport called "bumper-stickering." People who are into "b.s.-ing" fall into one of two classes, the collectors and the creators.

Collectors have a problem right off, which is that you can't actually take stickers home and hang them in your den, because they're attached to bumpers which are attached to cars. Even the owners can't get them off. They're stuck with them, you might say. Like an embarrassing tattoo, or a badly pierced ear. What you collect are the sayings, in a little notebook, or on the back of unused pledge cards.

Bumper-sticker collectors cherish originals, like the "Virginia is for lovers," from back in the sixties, or the daring "Sailors have more fun," or the original "Smile, God loves you." There's a special group who look for the ones that told the Ayatollah Khomeni what he could do. Another specialist group are the aficionados of the social consciousness series, like "Save the Whales," "Ban the Bomb," "Protect the Air," and "This truck pays $4,578.48 in taxes."

Collecting is probably fun, and at least as profitable as collecting swizzle sticks or old sermons; but the real artists among the "b.s.-ers" are the creators who think up such clever lines as "I'm pedaling as fast as I can," "This car stops at all garage sales," "Pennsylvania, Land of Taxes," and the gentlemanly "Same to you, buddy."

The top rank creators are those who can create *ad seriatim*, like the inventor of the famous "Honk if . . ." series. "Honk if you love country western . . . love yogurt . . . love your cat . . . love Jesus." "Honk if you are Irish . . . Polish . . . Hungarian . . . a grandmother." "Honk if you would rather be walking . . . are free for the evening." There's also the endless "I love (with a heart for the word 'love')" series. "I love New York

. . . Chicago . . .San Francisco . . . Vermont . . . Texas . . . South Philly . . . poodles . . . dobermans . . . parakeets . . . my horse . . . Reagan (a re-birth of the old 'I like Ike' slogan) . . . Friday . . . milk . . . Mario's pizza."

The newest "b.s.-ers" are people with an "I get no respect" syndrome. Like police cars telling us that "Our cops are tops." There's also "Firemen make house calls," "Nurses are caring people," "If you can read this, thank a teacher," and "If you had breakfast, thank a farmer." (Why not thank the chicken, or McDonalds?)

Sooner or later the church was bound to catch on. Usually we get there when everyone else is thinking of leaving. Last week I saw "Happiness is attending First Presbyterian." Seeing as how there are probably forty-seven First Presbyterians in our state, your chances of finding the happiness one are not great. At least, that's better than "In case of the rapture, this car will be unoccupied."

Some say "b.s.-ing" isn't biblical, but that's only because in those days they didn't have bumpers to put stickers on. Where do you paste a sticker on a donkey or a camel? That didn't keep some of them from having one ready in case they figured out where to attach it. There was Peter's "Fishermen make net profits," Noah's "Think snow," and Jonah's "You can't keep a good man down."

But, preachers are the original b.s. experts of the church, and some of us have our favorites. Like when I drive my gold-trimmed Mercedes convertible up that big I-95 in the sky, the people going the other way will read on the back, "I *tried* to tell you, but you wouldn't listen."

Doubt and Out

My rule about weeding has always been, "when in doubt — pull it out." I've exterminated some of my wife's prize wild flowers over the years, but she's a forgiving sort and we've managed to stay together.

There was a dentist we once went to who had the same "if in doubt, yank it out" philosophy. He was cheap, but if you stayed with him too long, you ended up with false teeth. Doctors back in the thirties were the same way about tonsils and adenoids. Take your child in with a broken arm or poison ivy, and he was likely to lose his tonsils and adenoids in the bargain. Doctors used to name their new cabin cruisers *T and A*.

My friend over at the Church of the Free Spirit says they have a similar rule about questionable members: "When in doubt — cast them out." They call it the "Jonah in the whale" rule. Most ministers have longed at least once for such a rule in their own denomination, but so far the only one in operation has been *about* ministers, not *for* ministers. ("For the sake of all concerned," intones the judicatory, "we believe Pastor So-and-so should seek a call to a new field of service.") In others words, "Pack, Mac." Very few may really know why, but that's just the point: There is doubt, so ship him out!

It doesn't matter whether the verb is pull, yank, cast, throw, ship, toss, drum, whatever, the message is in the two words "doubt" and "out." Wherever you have doubt, somebody's going to be out. Something about church life cannot bear doubt.

And something about human nature loves cleaning things out. I've saved many a lost day by at least cleaning out a few files. Makes you feel you've accomplished something. I don't subscribe to the slogan, "A clean desk means a clean mind." One of the smartest men I ever knew had such a jungle of an office that the sign on the door said, "Come in — I'm here somewhere." Nonetheless, there is undeniable satisfaction in seeing a weed-free garden, a clutter-free desk, or even a problem-free congregation.

A cleaned-out heaven is another matter, however. My Calvinist theology is that God has had his doubts about us ever since Adam and Eve bit the apple. God could easily play the "doubt-out" game, and most of us would be the outees. Heaven would be clean and serene, but it wouldn't mean much down where we would be.

The good news is that God has always been willing to give us the benefit of the doubt. "Forgive their sin and let them in," is his rule.

That won't change my ways with weeds in the garden, or the clutter in my files, but I expect it ought to make me look more tolerantly upon other people. As Matthew 7:2 says, "The *outment* with which you *out* will be the *outment* with which you are *outed*." And I sure don't want that.

The Clergy Nightmare

Ever since I have been a minister I have had this same dream. I am to be the preacher for a community service at the town's biggest church. People who have learned about it will come by the thousands just to hear me. My fellow clergy are so pleased that I will preach. They'll all be sitting in the front row taking notes. I've written one of the best sermons of my career, and it's all learned and ready. I set out for the church but get delayed by traffic, most of it headed for the church. It's now only five minutes till starting time and I'm stuck at a red light. I'll make it, and the sermon is all ready, so "not to worry, luv." At just two minutes before the hour, I arrive at the church. The parking lot is jammed and there is a line of people waiting to get in the door of the church. I park in the clergy space and calmly walk inside, waving to people on the way. Inside, the host pastor and choir are already lined up. I nod and smile and say in a firm voice, "Okay, let's go." They don't move. They're all staring at my legs. I forgot my pants!

I've often wondered whether all preachers have that dream. Maybe each one has his own version. My friend over at the Church of the Free Spirit says that in his dream he arrives as guest preacher, the church is full of his fellow free spirits, and just as he walks in and takes his seat behind the pulpit, he realizes that he doesn't have his sermon! He admits that he isn't sure in his heart that the Great Free Spirit in the Sky is going to put the words into his mouth, so he is glad when his wife wakens him and says, "Will you please stop that groaning!"

I asked the rabbi over at Beth Kosher Synagogue, and he confessed that he's dreamed so often about showing up for Friday evening service without his yarmulke that he keeps a spare one under the lectern. I've noticed that he also keeps one in his car, along with his paperback copy of *1,000 One-liners from Henny Youngman*.

So the clergy nightmare is ecumenical. I wonder, though, if the plots may be denominational. A priest dreams that he is all ready to start the Mass and he suddenly can't remember a word of Latin. A Baptist minister dreams that he is leading a convert down into the tank and somebody forgot to warm up the water. A Christian Science practitioner dreams that he keeps referring to Mary Aker Beddy. Even the Moslem muezzin dreams of climbing to the top of his minaret at the hour of prayer and forgetting which way is Mecca.

Maybe all these nightmares are our "thorn in the flesh," which Paul said God gives us to keep us humble. Nothing does a better job of keeping you humble than showing up in church without your pants. That may also be why the pulpit robe was invented.

Some people would probably say that it's a lack of faith to worry about those dreams. "Don't you believe Luke 12:12?" they would ask in their best Bible-believing tone of voice. "If ever you do show up without your sermon or your pants, 'the Holy Spirit will teach you in that very hour what you ought to say.'" I can't imagine what it would be. I'd really rather have the Holy Spirit tell me, "Relax, Paul, it'll never happen as long as I am in the Trinity."

I am consoled in all this by the fact that when I join that big Ministerium in the Sky, there won't be any bad dreams. In fact, there won't be trousers, only white robes and golden wings. That's another of my bad dreams. I arrive and go to get my wings, and they have only thirty-fours and thirty-sixes. I'm a thirty-five! I hope the Holy Spirit will have something appropriate for me to say then.

Ho-Ha-88

Our Session is ambidextrous; we've got both men and women. There are eight of the former and seven of the latter, which arrangement sometimes causes split votes, as it did just last week on a motion to allow liturgical dancing in church. Remembering the black leotards the young lady dancers wore the last time, the Session voted eight for and seven against.

The appearance of the dance team is to be part of a time of liturgical celebration planned to liven up the post-Epiphany, pre-Lenten slump. There will be folk singing, clowning, homemade poetry, maybe even tumblers and jugglers. "HolyHappy-88," the Session decided to call it, after rejecting Liturgication, Celeration, Lit-Cel-O-Rama, and one caustic suggestion that it be called the February Follies. ("Why don't we just wear funny hats and tell jokes," a critic suggested.)

But let me back up a bit. It all started when some members complained to the Worship Committee that they felt left out of things. "Only the preacher and the choir and an occasional lost starling ever get to do anything creative on Sunday mornings," they said. "People should be able to use their talents, not bury them like the man in the parable." As soon as you quote the Bible like that, our Session snaps to. Immediately, they appointed a committee to make a survey of the membership. They found out that there are all sorts of talents in the church, and people want to see them used to the glory of the Lord — no holds barred.

There were some specific suggestions, too. "Take my George," one lady wrote. "He can't carry a tune in a bucket, but since he's been retired, he's got quite good at painting by the numbers. He could do a real nice Head of John the Baptizer, if you would just find a place in the service for him." Another member said that he would like to play the offertory on his musical saw. The only thing he knows is Mother Machree, but we agreed that that's kind of religious, and done on a saw is slow enough to allow the ushers time to get all the way to the back.

One man related how the church where they went before he transferred here had an annual Blessing of the Hobbies service in January. He said it always drew a big crowd, which the Session took advantage of by having the annual special mission offering that day.

A number of men suggested, "Why don't you have those liturgical dancers again?"

So we're off and running with Ho-Ha-88, as we call it for short. George is going to do his "Head of John the Baptizer" in place of the sermon. Our saw virtuoso is learning "Danny Boy" from his *You, Too, Can Play Irish Favorites* book as an encore, in case we have a slow team of ushers that day. And our Computers for Jesus club plans to praise the Lord by programing all the forms of iniquity listed in the Old Testament and all the corresponding forgivenesses in the New Testament, and doing a readout on the whole thing in place of the prayer of confession and the assurance of pardon.

The committee is making sure that no one who wants to take part will be left out, even if we have to stretch the theology a bit. For example, when one dear lady lamented, "I can't do anything special; I'm just a housewife," we declared cooking and cleaning to be God-given talents, and now she's going to take up the offering with her Electrolux. Another "just-a-housewife" is going to move her microwave into the chancel and make a loaves-and-fishes souffle right in front of the reredos. "If they can dance the Psalms in those leotards," she sniffed, "I can certainly bake the Gospels in my apron." The senior highs have formed a Bible rock group and have even composed an original number in honor of God, called "Hey, Man, Like You're Really It, Ya Know?"

> *Hey, Man, like you're really it, ya know, ya know?*
> *And I'm really like zilch, ya know, ya know?*
> *But you don't basically care, ya know, ya know?*
> *You still want me up there, ya know, ya know?*
> *Awesome.*

When I told my friend over at the Church of the Free Spirit what we were doing, I could see him turning green with envy. They thought they had the winner in their New Year's Day "Meals of All Nations" potluck supper for the hunger fund. They've never seen those black leotards.

Pew Pencils

People are always saying that we should see what works in other churches and borrow it for our church. I hope they don't mean the minister. Anyway, I've being going around to see what I can find out, and I've come to one conclusion. It's the pencils that matter. Someone is always writing an article on how important it is for ushers to remember that they make the first impression on visitors, but the pew pencils are the real evangelists.

You go into a church and sit in the pew before the service, and the first thing you do is look to see what's in the pew rack for you to scribble with when the sermon comes. Now, if it's an up-and-coming church, you'll know right away from the pencil. A nice, long pencil with a good point and the words, "Welcome to First Church. We preach the true Gospel," printed in gold on it will tell you that this church means business. Oh, maybe it doesn't hurt if the message is "Compliments of Ace Funeral Home: We'll be the last to let you down," but give me a church that gets its own message across, like "We are a friendly church," or "Ham and oyster suppers our specialty." As that old inscriber Moses said, "It's the point that makes the pencil, but it's also the pencil that makes the point." (Exodus 41:1)

Anyway, look around at the other pews, and if the pencils are all uniform, all sticking up like little soldiers of the Lord ready to serve, it means you're in a church that pays attention to details. They probably pick up all the old bulletins from last week's service and check under the pews for chewing gum. Over their narthex door are the words, "Cleanliness is next to godliness." (Proverbs 31:32)

On the other hand, if the pencils are a "duke's mixture" of red, blue, green, and yellow stubs, some hardly long enough to stick up out of the hole, and most of them with broken points and chewed-up sides, it could mean that this is a family-type church with kids. That tells you what to expect; like babies crying, little girls wanting to go out to the bathroom during the sermon, and voices that pipe up with things like "Mommy, who's he talking to?" when the preacher is praying. Beware of a church with unkempt pencils, if it's peace and quiet you want.

One of the things you want a pencil for is to mark the little squares on the visitor's card. This is how a church knows you were there, so they can send you a "Glad-you-were-here-please-come-again" letter. It also gives you a chance to say you would like a call from the pastor, would like the pastor to stick to the Bible, or wish they would sing some of the old hymns, like "Church in the Wildwood" or "Whispering Hope."

One church where I stopped to do some research had those little cards with the pink "VISITOR" pin attached. It was a Wednesday afternoon and no one was around, so I took the pin for further study, signed my name and address on the card, and put it back into the holder. About a week later I received a letter from the minister saying how nice it was to see me there and he hoped I liked the sermon. I wrote back that it was the best sermon I ever heard, and I was sorry more people weren't there to hear it.

A church I served way back in my career may or may not have had good pencils, I don't remember, but it had Marvin. Marvin was our coffee-pourer. "Never on Sunday" was his policy about church going. You wouldn't even see him on Christmas and Easter. He only came to church when there was a supper. Then Marvin poured coffee. Something about going around keeping the cups filled spoke to Marvin's soul. His eyes glowed, his face smiled, he spoke a cheery word to everyone, and called everyone "Brother" or "Sister" in the best evangelical fashion. When Marvin gets to heaven, the saints that have gone marching in will at least know they'll get a good cup of coffee. Hell is where you can't count on that.

I put Marvin in a class with good pew pencils. They both make the right impression on strangers, and that's where evangelism begins. I don't care if the Lord doesn't greet me in heaven with a three-points-and-a-poem sermon, but if he gives me a good cup of coffee and a sharp pencil, I'll write the nicest glad-to-be-here note you ever saw in that big Ritual of Friendship book in the sky.

Boggles and Bagels

My mind is boggled so often anymore that it no longer knows a boggle from a bagel. People do such things that I simply fall into a state of mental floundering when I try to comprehend.

I look at a tall, gleaming, new hotel and convention center, and try to think how one man can design all those millions of angles, and corners, and jointures, and stress curves, and then be so right that he can say, "Go ahead, build it. It'll stand up." The mind boggles.

People put out such numbers that the brain is stunned. Forty-five billion, for instance. Can you picture forty-five billion anythings? I had to look up billion, and discovered that Webster's Collegiate doesn't even try to define it, but refers the reader to "the numbers table" on page 479, where they run it out in digits — words failing, I suppose. A billion is 1,000,000,000.

And what's the 45,000,000,000? That is the number of paper and plastic cups we throw in the trash every year! The brain reels. And that's along with 21,000,000,000 plastic dishes and bowls, 15,000,000,000 paper plates, and 18,000,000,000 plastic lids. We're building our own "tower with its top in the heavens," not in Babel, but out of the debris of what must be one big, year-long picnic going on somewhere. We also bury, bundle, or burn 16,000,000,000 disposable diapers, and scatter across the earth 2,000,000,000 razors and razor blades. I'll never go barefoot again.

Maybe I just have an easily boggled mind. I even have trouble understanding how my camera knows the difference between one-tenth and one-hundredth of a second. I know that if a second has hundredths, it must have a hundred of them, but how can that little piece of Japanese plastic, glass, and springs separate one of them from the other ninety-nine? How can a stopwatch tell that Mary Decker Slaney ran the mile just two-hundredths of a second faster than the last time? The material in her track shirt would make more difference than that. Such things dazzle my razzle.

I'm hearing something else, like another message from somewhere familiar, something about boggle and dazzle and God. It's that old Psalmist friend of mine saying,

> When I look at the stars, the sun and moon which thou has made, what is man, that thou art mindful of him?

I join his boggle. Six million stars in just one corner of a galaxy, and a million galaxies so far away that it'll take a million years for the light from one of them to show up in my evening sky some winter night. And God, who made all this, cares more about us than about all that! There's boggle for you — God the great boggler of man's mind!

And he doesn't quit with that. Here's where it really hits me. My mind falters and staggers and can hardly go on when I try to think how men could make themselves take a mallet, drive nails through the gristle and bone of men's hands and feet, and then hang them up on crosses along the roads of their empire, and call it *Pax*; and that 2,000 years later my life is affected profoundly by one of those crosses, the one with the young rabbi from Nazareth on it. And he's called by all men the Prince of Pax!

It boggles the mind. Thank God it also saves my soul.

Shortspeak

A friend from the ministerium called to ask me to take part in a community service. He said they would like me to read the bibes. I asked him if that was anything like the banns, and who was getting married. It turned out that he meant the Bible selections. I told him that I would rather do the invo, or maybe pronounce the benie.

This isn't some new glossolalia; it's just the church keeping up with the times. We may not be of this world, but we sure don't want anybody to think we're not with it. And to be with the world these days you have to know how to use shortspeak, like "nuke 'em" for "drop a nuclear bomb on them and annilhilate their country." Look at the time you save, as well as the wear and tear on your voice box. In the case of "nuke 'em," it also saves you some unpleasant images. That's one of the best things about shortspeak.

Shortspeak should not be confused with alliteration, nor even abbreviation. Neither of these is man at his intellectual best, but at least they don't coin words that are as charming as a newly-tarred road. Shortspeak, on the other hand, has us saying things like "condo," "veggie," "networking," and "blurb." Energy-effective as they may be, where's the romance in such words? Where's the music? the color? the dreamy images? Cantaloupe always made me think of a sun-washed isle off the coast of Mexico, but "lopes" on my grocer's handbill sounds like a burp in print. And his "cukes" for cucumbers is a misconceived notion of cleverness, like calling Dom Perignon "booze," like saying "shhh" for "pianissimo," or like shortening "the Kingdom of Heaven" to "God's Condo."

The jewel in the crown of shortspeak is "into," as in "George is into water-colors," "Margaret is into tofu," "old Dr. Smith is into expository preaching," "Jonah was into whales." A rock singer, who was being interviewed on TV the other night, said that he used to be "into drugs," but now he's "into God." The next morning God interrupted my devotionals to ask, "Paul, who is this guy, anyway, and how did he get green hair?" I had to answer, "Lord, I can't help you on that; I'm not into rock stars."

Our trustees, who are into deficit financing, decided to see if shortspeak might help. They took up the question with the Prayers-R-Us Bible Class. They're usually the cutting edge of our congregation. If something goes with the PRUs, we always say, it'll probably play down the hall at the Ladies' Brotherhood.

The PRUs said, "Give it a shot." They thought we could start with chairman, which is usually abbreviated "Chm." and pronounced the way a Pennsylvania Dutchman says Jim. For starters, they shortspoke Christian Education Chm. to "Cejim," gave us "Wojim" for Worship Chm., "Stewjim" for Stewardship Chm., and "Jimmish" for Chm. of Missions. The church calendar next week could read, "There will be a joint meeting on Wednesday evening of the Cejim, Wojim, Stewjim, and Jimmish in the Rec. Hall." For churches that have commissions instead of committees, the PRUs suggested "Spife" for the Commission on Spiritual Life, "Pife" for Parish Life, "Wife" for Worship Life, and "Strife" for — what else? — Stewardship Life.

Useful to the church as it may be, shortspeak is probably just another fad, and we shouldn't get too far into it. You might say it isn't carved in stone. It probably isn't biblical, either. In fact, the Bible is definitely longspeak. Take David. David used a hundred and thirteen R.S.V. words to describe God as a shepherd, and most people remember every one of them. Paul went on for two hundred and fifty words just to say that love is best of all. The bottom line seems to be: Shortspeak for bulletins, longspeak for Bibles. It's probably because God has more time than people do, and maybe more beauty in his soul.

Pewology

Pews are more noticeable in the summertime when so many of them are empty. Maybe you've been noticing some of yours and wondering where the idea of pews came from and why only the church has them, and things like that. So as a special end-of-summer treat, here's a short lesson in pewology.

Back in the days of Martin Luther, John Calvin, and John Knox, people who attended church had to stand through the entire time. And the services were hours long! There is certain to be a reason for this somewhere in church history, but it doesn't come immediately to mind. Perhaps seating technology hadn't developed far enough, and standing was state-of-the-art. A truly sorry state-of-the-art, we would say, but for centuries standing in church was *de rigueur*.

Nobody knows who was the first person to hew a pew, but when seats finally did arrive in churches, a lot of problems came with them. For one thing, there was the question of what to call them. Lecterns were elevated to "pulpits," robes were changed to "vestments," and even songs were re-christened "hymns." (A good thing, too. Can you imagine announcing "responsive reading fourteen in the back of the songnal?") So you couldn't just keep calling seats "seats."

It was finally decided that since the seats were really benches that rested on carved feet, they be named after the old medieval word for feet, which was *puie*. A lot of old medieval feet probably deserved the word, but it wasn't fitting for use in church, so they changed the spelling to the slightly less demonstrative *pew*. (They also quietly re-instituted the ritual of foot-washing.)

This was no sooner cleaned up when a disagreement arose over when to use the pews. Calvin, in a rare light-hearted moment of rhyming, wrote,

*Use the pews when it's time to pray,
but standing's the thing when it's time to sing.*

Anglicans were horrified at such crudeness and shot right back,

That'll be the day, when WE sit to pray.

Anglicans also liked to say, "The only good prayer is a knelt prayer." If you must sit, they said, do it when you read the Scriptures. Anglicans were still pretty much of the old school and secretly believed that "no pews is good pews."

Lutherans seemed to like the going up and down more than either the actual sitting or standing. For them, a pew was just a stopping off place between risings and sittings. The Anabaptists and Pietists had no strong feelings one way or the other. As long as you go all the way under when you are baptized, standing or sitting doesn't mean a thing in the end, they held. Of course, they didn't have long sermons and were more often on their knees than on their ends.

The only thing the Bible says is that a man should not "stand in the company of sinners, nor sit in the seat of the scornful." Of course, anyone that perfect wouldn't really need to go to church in the first place.

Some pews come equipped with pew cushions, which some rigorists decry as decadent and lending too much "ease in Zion." We overcame that problem by vowing to give up our cushions each year during Lent. After the first time, we had to put suction cups on the bottoms of the cushions because our sexton decided to wax the pews while the cushions were off, and after-Lent worshipers were sliding right out of sight.

We may as well get used to pews, because we'll always have them, even in heaven. As the good book says, "Sinners shall not stand in the judgment," and I suspect that means this man-in-the-pulpit, as well as most of you-in-the-pew.

The Van Advantage

The ad in the church supplies magazine said,

We put the van into evangelical.

It was from a company that sells buses and other vehicles to churches. "With your church's logo and a brief message tastefully lettered on its side panels, your van becomes a rolling instrument of salvation," they promised.

Think of that! The outdoor sign, the faithful old wayside pulpit, has met its match. For decades these metal messengers of the Lord have called the passing world to pause and read eternal truths.

You stand tallest when you are on your knees.

The more smiles you give, the more smiles you get.

With sacred succinctness, in obedience to Habakkuk's command, they made the vision plain, that he may run who readeth.

CH-CH. What's missing? UR

And now they want us to give them up for a Dodge Ram. Well, I may be a sentimentalist, but I don't think the side panel of a van can ever equal the appeal of a wayside pulpit telling me the good news I'm longing to hear,

Covered Dish Supper
Sunday, 5:00 PM
All welcome

But progress must be served. It will be a gradual phaseout, but the old rugged sign is headed for that big museum in the sky, where it will take its place beside the mimeograph, funeral parlor fan, and the every member canvass. So join me in a farewell salute to a faithful servant.

> *Oh, that old rugged sign,*
> *Now replaced by a Ford,*
> *Had a wondrous attraction for me.*
> *For 'twas on that dear sign,*
> *That the words were displayed,*
> *That said, "Rummage sale from nine till three."*
>
> *So I'll cherish the old rugged sign,*
> *Till there are no more covered dish meals.*
> *I'll remember the old rugged sign,*
> *But exchange it for something on wheels.*

Farewell, Model 712 — The Westminster. Adieu, Model Q47-T — The Genevan. Auf wiedersehen, Model CS 206 — The Calvin Special, "with gothic lettering and rust-proof frame." A new day is dawning, the day of the Vagabond, the four-wheel drive Adventurer, the twelve-passenger Traveler with turbo drive and air conditioning.

In all fairness, it must be said that a van has its (you'll forgive the expression) ad*v*antages. For instance, it gives you four message panels for the price of one. You have the two sides, where you can put your church's name and an attractive message like

First Presbyterian Church
Where a Warm Welcome is Predestined

Across the front you can letter "sevas suseJ" backwards, the way they do on ambulances. And on the back you can put,

Follow me, I'm on my way to heaven

(I once followed a car that had that on a bumper sticker and wound up at Denny's Restaurant.)

All kinds of churches can use vans. In our town the Seventh Day Adventists have one that has "Closed Sundays" painted on its side. There's one at the Catholic parish that is usually full of nuns and is known affectionately as The Gregorian Greyhound. The synagogue has a van which they call the Car Mitzvah, and even the local atheists drive around in an unmarked van.

Vans also distinguish you from the fundamentalists. They always have buses. The reason they have to use buses is that they have to haul more people. The reason they have more people is that they cheat! They don't develop mission designs, except a crude "go out and bring them in." They don't hold nearly the requisite number of committee meetings nor appoint proper commissions. They neglect to write position papers and resolutions, and most of them haven't had a decent reorganization in fifty years. They're shamefully irresponsible, and their loaded buses give them away. But a van tells the world that your church plays by the rules. And don't forget, in the Father's house may be many rooms, but the parking is limited. Vans will park where buses fear to tread.

If you can't afford a van, and even your wayside pulpit has fallen apart, be not dismayed. Look what Peter did with only a pair of sandals and a heart of love.

"Do You Speak . . . ?"

The young man coming toward me in front of the feed store had on a yellow T-shirt that said in blue letters, "I speak farming."
"Say something in farming," I greeted him.
"Bank loans, price supports, interest rates," he recited.
Hmmm.
The athletic-looking fellow passing me in front of the stadium had on a T-shirt that said, "I speak baseball."
"Say something in baseball," I called after him.
"Free agent, bonus, endorsements," he called back over his shoulder.
Figures.
The woman sitting next to me at the PTA meeting had on a T-shirt that said, "I speak teaching."
"Say something in teaching," I asked of her.
"Contract, salary schedule, tenure," she responded.
Okay.
I tried it on my doctor. "Say something in doctor," I suggested to him. "I mean *real* doctor, not the technical talk you use in front of your nurse."
Without batting an eye, he came back with "Tax shelter, stock options, malpractice insurance."
"There's a pattern developing here," I said to myself in that confidential tone of voice I use when I say things to myself. "Let's try a few more."
I went to my lawyer. "Say something in lawyer," I asked of him.
"Retainer, percentage of award, court costs," he replied.
"I think he's got it," I sang. "He's really got it!"
Now for the test: a minister. Ministers aren't known for being state-of-the-art. Let's see how they do. I asked the wearer of a clerical collar sitting in front of me at presbytery, "Do you speak clergy?"

"Could Moses count to ten?" he shot back.

"So, speak some clergy for me," I asked anxiously.

"Minimum salary, car allowance, tax deduction," he answered.

I needn't have worried.

So, relax. This old world knows where it's at, knows which side of the bread is buttered, knows where the cookie will crumble. We've got our feet on the ground, our heads screwed on right, our eyes squarely on the bottom line. The children of this world are no longer wiser in their generation than the children of light. In fact, they all seem to be the same people. God's in his heaven; all's right with the world.

And yet . . .

I placed a call to Saint Peter (you just dial 1-800-UPTHERE). They put me on hold for a while. I listened to the Mormon Tabernacle Choir singing "America the Beautiful." When Peter finally came on the line, I asked him, "Sir, do you speak Heavenly?"

"Why, yes, I do," he answered, with a "Smile, God loves you" in his voice. "Why do you ask?"

"Would you say something in Heavenly for me?" I asked.

"Love, joy, peace," he sang, "give, trust, believe."

Uh-oh.

Spider, Spider, on the Mike

During the sermon a few Sundays ago, a little black spider dropped down from the end of the microphone and hung suspended right above Ezekiel's wheels. Ordinarily, I can take spiders or leave them alone, depending on how they take me, but in the middle of a sermon, I don't need any more distraction. I get enough from helicopters, sirens, coughers and book-droppers — and people who sit there grinning and I can't figure out why.

If there's anything a preacher who has already lost his way doesn't need, it's wandering punctuation. I couldn't be sure whether this spider had in mind just to hang there peacefully or drop down and become a moving comma on my notes. Just as bad, he might go back up his little cable into the microphone and cause sounds to come out that didn't originate with me. It's enough that I have to keep explaining what I say every week without having to explain spider noises. He may have been one of the Lord's little creatures, but he was not my favorite at the moment.

For a while, he just stayed there, hanging on my every word, you might say — or you might not say, because my words have never been hung on by anybody that I know of. They've come close to hanging me from time to time, but that's another matter.

At any rate, about midway through point three of the sermon, the spider made his move. At first, I lost sight of him. If there's anything more unnerving than seeing a spider in front of your nose, it's seeing a spider in front of your nose and then suddenly *not* seeing it. When you've got a nose as big as mine, you'd better locate him quickly. I did; he was making his way across from Ezekiel's wheels to the Valley of Dry Bones. Actually, it was the valley between the two halves of the Bible. If you must know the truth, I thought about making the valley that of a certain spider's dry bones. At that instant, my newest hymn came to mind:

Little spider I am liable,
  To slam shut that pulpit Bible;
Or I might just poke my finger,
  Right where you have stopped to linger,
So, little spider, move a bit faster,
  Before you get sent to meet your Master.

(refrain)
Alleluia, alleluia, alleluia,
  praise the Lord.

And that's how new hymns get written. I mean, you didn't think someone sits down and says, "Come now and forsooth, let us beget a new hymn." Oh, no, they come by inspiration, unbidden, like the time the Rev. George Duffield fell off his horse on the way to church and by the time he arrived, he had written the opening hymn, "Stand up, stand up, for Jesus." Necessity is the mother of much spirit-leading.

The spider may not have cared about my threats, but he did reverse course and crawl up on the back of my hand. I tried to brush him off and succeeded in brushing page six right off onto the floor. Maybe you noticed that the sermon that day had only two-and-a-half points, and you got out ten minutes early. Don't be so happy; you missed my grand finale, where I really demolished Jerry Falwell and the whole Moral Majority, proved my mastery of Greek and Hebrew, and recited twenty-seven stanzas of Edgar Guest's "I Always Pay My Pledge on Time."

I'll tell you, it just doesn't pay to miss church around here. You never know what's going to happen. Next Sunday might be the best one yet.

Gift Horses

Things have been in a snit at the Finance Committee meetings recently, due to the fact that the television set in the church lounge went bad and there is no money in the budget to replace it. The right wing conservatives on the committee see it as no less than a major theological issue. "It's a sign from God that television is not a proper thing to have in the church," they declare. "The Lord hath spoken; woe unto him who heedeth not." They always talk in King James like that when they're being theological.

The moderates aren't sure they approve of the television either, but they think they should vote for it in principle and decide about appropriating the funds later on. "That way it can be a bargaining chip," they explain. I know more about chocolate chips than bargaining chips, but I think I recognize their way of being for, against, and neither one, all at the same time. Moderates like to be everyone's friend.

The liberals want to go ahead and buy a new TV and pay for it by placing a verifiable freeze on Sunday School Easter parties. They argue that the money saved on chocolate crosses and the Easter bunny suit would be more than enough for a new TV. "Kids these days don't believe in the Easter bunny anyway," they declare. This causes the conservatives to rend their garments and cry, "Blasphemy!" and the moderates to wring their hands and plead for compromise. "Maybe we could settle for hollow chocolate and just repairing the old TV," they suggest. Moderates want to keep everybody happy.

Which, by the way, is how we got the TV in the first place. One of our families bought a new one with cable and remote and VCR, and they wanted a decent way of getting rid of the old one. It wasn't that the TV store wanted ten dollars to haul it away that they said, "No, let's give it to the church." They simply felt that the church ought to have a TV set and this one was "only twelve years old and still has a lot of good use in it," and it would make them feel good to know that the church had it.

The Property Committee wanted to say, "No, thanks," because they had looked too many gift horses in the mouth and seen the cavities; but the Membership Committee was afraid of offending the family and maybe sending them to the Methodist Church down the street. "If it will keep them happy, isn't that what the church is for?" they argued. So, we kept them happy. In fact, we've kept so many people happy that the church is beginning to look like a museum.

Which is also how the Sunday church school got that big yellow piano with the cracked sounding board. One of our families was refurnishing their rec room, after the water had gotten in, and there was this piano. "It belonged to my great aunt," said the wife, "and I know she would want the church to have it. She went to a Presbyterian church when she was a girl."

"It will sag the floor," protested the Property Committee. "It will keep them happy," recited the Membership Committee. "I don't have room for another piano," cried the Sunday church school superintendent. "Well, they're regular pledgers," announced the Stewardship Committee. That usually settles the hash.

One of the things I remember from Hebrew class in seminary is the word *genizah*, which means the place where old copies of the Torah are stored in the synagogue, because who wants to throw away a Torah scroll? It's like who wants to throw away the old family Bible when it doesn't fit in with the decor of the new house. Give it to the church. Where else should old Bibles go to die? Sometimes I think our church has become the *genizah* for old Bibles, and TVs, pianos, ceramic statues, old paintings, worn-out rugs, and the former minister's collection of General Assembly Minutes. Maybe we should put a sign over the door,

>   *Give me your tired, your poor . . .*

That might even mean some of us.

You Are What You Eat

Our student assistant began his sermon a few weeks ago with the suggestion that we think of what kind of food we would like to be, if we were going to be food instead of people. The first thing that came to my mind was the nutritionist's slogan, "You are what you eat."

Does that mean I'm a bowl of All-Bran?

Actually, I'd rather be a crab casserole with cheddar cheese sauce. I want to be loved. I used to think that as a clergyman I was gourmet food at bargain prices. Now I feel more like aging food, but I am consoled by the fact that the older cheese gets, the sharper it gets, and old wine is always best, even if it isn't bursting many wineskins anymore.

Some clergymen are Egg Foo Young; you can't figure them out. Some think they are chicken soup, good for whatever ails you. I could be stewed prunes, just to keep you active. I always considered my sermons soul food, but some people have been ingracious enough to suggest that they are really junk food. The legendary Satchel Paige once said that you should never eat fried food because "it angers the stomach." Sometimes I'm fried food to the Session, but if I get them home by ten they forgive and forget.

All this about food makes you wonder whether the church was born with a menu for its first Bible. We do know that it all began with an apple, and it does seem that we manage to eat something at just about every event we have in the church. Sometimes I wonder if Jesus didn't say, "Behold, the potluck supper is at hand, repent ye!" Some of us have been repenting after potluck suppers for a long time now. The children of Israel got through the wilderness on frequent imbibements of manna and quail, which caused them such serious gastric repentence that Moses had to go out and get them some tablets. Jacob and Esau split up over a bowl of red stew, which sounds like it could split up anybody. John the Baptizer invented the Jordan River diet of locusts and wild honey, and you wouldn't believe the pages of recipes and directions the Bible has for keeping kosher.

It's a long way from Eve's offer of an apple to the Ladies Aid bake sale and quilt raffle, but it all seems to be on the same text: "Love the Lord your God with all your heart, and all your soul, and all your appetite, and your cookbook as yourself." I never knew a church that didn't have a book of favorite recipes to sell along with its tracts and Bible portions. Right there beside the Ten Commandments and the Beatitudes we grew up learning Aunt Mary's favorite recipe for seven-bean salad and tuna surprise. We teach the toddlers in the nursery to eat cookies even before we have them singing "Jesus Wants Me for a Sunbeam." Even the rookie preacher learns to get his sermon finished before all the pot roasts in the congregation start to burn. The Lord's army does indeed seem to travel on its stomach.

So I guess that when the egg roll is called up yonder, we'll all be there, chomping and munching and sipping and wondering if there will be seconds. Of course, the only reason we'll make it at all is that Jesus himself wanted to be food. He took bread and broke it, and a cup of wine and held it up, and he said, "Here's what I am . . . for you." Without that we would all be on the outside of the banquet hall looking in.

Burnout

Want to know what controversial subject ministers are talking about behind closed doors these days? Sure you do.

It's "burnout" . . . really. We're becoming obsessed with the danger of burning out, like an old light bulb or a used up candle stub. You've heard the song, "Old Preachers Never Die, They Just Sputter Away." It's become our haunting melody. Time was when all a clergyman had to avoid was heresy, blasphemy, and martyrdom.

Now comes "burnout," and all previous occupational hazards pale in comparison. The glassy stare, the mumbled response, the abbreviated sermon, the lack of enthusiasm for covered dish suppers, are symptoms of a modern mal-de-cleric that's spreading amongst the persons of the cloth.

Let me show you how serious this is. Last week I opened a just-arrived publisher's catalog, and on the page called "For the Pastor" eight of the twelve books were on burnout, two were on ministerial tax loopholes, one on buying at discount, and one on counseling the bereaved. If the power of suggestion works, we can look for a lot of zombied reverends next year, at least among those who read books. Just reading eight books in a year has been known to cause permanent trauma in some clergypersons.

But the bottom line is, "What's the solution to 'burnout'?" Well, some suggest "hide out." Get some secret place and hide out there till the pressure is off. If this catches on, I predict a sharp jump in the number of ministerial retreats to such remote study centers as the Sands, the Bermuda Hilton, or the Club Caribbe.

Some have escaped simply by "dropping out." They leave the pastorate and go to fundraising, or take up chicken farming, or necktie painting. Most are quickly healed by the first reminder from the Board of Pensions.

I doubt that the burnout craze will last long. Sooner or later someone's going to remind us of how Isaiah said you could manage to "mount up with wings like eagles, run and not be weary, walk and not faint." But at least let us have a week at the Club Caribbe before you tell us, okay?

Let Us Pray . . .

The debate over prayer in the schools raises some serious questions about just how far we should let this sort of thing go. Once it's okay in the classroom, can we keep them from praying in the cafeteria?

Oh Lord, deliver us from the destruction that wasteth at noonday.

Or teachers from praying in the faculty lounge?

Oh Lord, give us peace.

Or cheerleaders from chanting in the stadium?

Rah, rah, rah — Sis, boom bah;
God's on our side — Ha, ha, ha.

I wonder if the sponsors of the prayer amendment realize what a pandora's box they're opening. I mean, if they pass this thing, you'll see people wanting to pray all over the place. America is a democracy, and that means equal rights, and that means that if they can pray in the school, we can pray in the supermarket.

Bless this store, O Lord, we pray,
Keep it open night and day;
And if it's not too much trouble,
Keep its coupons always double.

And if in the supermarket, why not the shopping center?

I was glad when they said unto me,
"Let us go over to the K-mart.
Our feet are standing at thy gates, O Woolco."

And if at the shopping center, why not at the mall?

> *Bless the mall, Oh my soul,*
> *And forget not all its parking space.*

There's no stopping it, once you let the cork out of the bottle.

Some of us may have actually jumped the gun on this. I was asked to pray at the dedication of a new swim club. It never occurred to me to check with the Supreme Court before I went there and prayed,

> *God is great and God is cool,*
> *And we thank him for this pool.*

I don't think my neighbor did either, before he sent his kids off to tennis camp, praying,

> *I would rather be a McEnroe on the courts of the Lord,*
> *Than to dwell on the greens at the country club.*

Some people are praying that the law won't pass, but I can't see why anybody would be against something as American as prayer. This country was born in prayer. General George Washington went up there to Valley Forge park and prayed us to victory over the British, who were also praying, but they didn't have the true faith. True faith always wins, and America is the land of true faith, as well as true grit, true love, and True toothpaste.

So, let us all pray. We'll start with the Lord's prayer, because everyone can say that — unless you happen to be one of those 5,900,000 Jews, 300,000 Muslims, 565,000 Jehovah's Witnesses, or 200,000 Buddhists, Baha'is, and who knows what all, who are Americans. In which case you can just sit quiet while the rest of us exercise our God-given right. Like I said, America is a democracy, and nobody can deny you the right to be a heathen, if that is your pleasure.

Thus May Become So

If you care at all about the dinosaurs, you will be as shocked as I was to learn that they didn't pass into slow, peaceful extinction the way the evolutionists told us. They were all killed by falling stars! Yes, those twinkle, twinkle little stars we used to make wishes on and tell our sweethearts their eyes sparkled like. Well, they aren't nice at all, they're killers of innocent mammals, of which, I remind you, we are a breed. So, learn to say,

> Star light, star bright,
> First bright star I've seen tonight,
> Wish I may, wish I might,
> Not get zapped by you tonight.

This whole cheerful gefilte fish comes to us from the researchers out at the University of California at Berkeley who keep watch on such important matters as how dinosaurs get dandruff, and the life cycles of creepy-crawlies. And it's no comfort that some of their colleagues disagree with them, because the Berkeleyites say their evidence is "overwhelming." They're sure. And they warn us that there is a super-killer star named Nemesis still floating around out there somewhere just watching, waiting. Maybe Big Brother is really Big Star, and he's out to get us all, us who always believed so much in the stars.

So, there goes another nail into the coffin of faith. If you can't trust your lucky stars, who can you trust? Certainly not Darwin. (And him so sure and all.) Probably not Einstein, either, nor Freud, Johnny Carson, Dear Abby, Ronald McDonald, nor any of the people we've relied on to tell us how it really is. Not one of them told us how it was with the dinosaurs. Didn't they know the truth?

"Ah," sighed Pontius Pilate, "Truth? What is truth?" He may have been smarter than he knew. In his day it was true that the world was flat. Science proved it. Then it was true that it was round. Columbus proved it. Now it is true that it egg-shaped and about to be scrambled and fried by bombs that some say it is true to call "peace keepers!" True keeps changing. It was true that you made money the old-fashioned way, you earned it; now you do it by winning the lottery. It was true that football was for autumn; now it's for spring; an apple kept the doctor away; now it computes his bill. You were right, old Pontius. "What *is* truth?" It depends upon what day it is.

Maybe the truth is that truth isn't. It's only provisional. It's true today and gone tomorrow, and everything is up for grabs. It's just like it says in Psalm 200,

> *This may become that, thus may become so,*
> *Here may become there, yes become no.*
> *Chocolate become tuna salad, coffee become tea,*
> *Honesty the worst policy, one and one three.*
>
> *Up become down, day become night,*
> *Over become under, left become right.*
> *Poor may become wealthy, rich become poor,*
> *Everything's so uncertain, that's all that's for sure.*
>   *Selah.*

Ah, but wait! The bottom line is that God is still in his heaven, and Hebrews 13:8 is still in the New Testament. At least, it was last week. You don't suppose that He . . . ? Nah, She wouldn't.

Your Own Personal Star

There are 200 billion stars in the Milky Way. (The galaxy, not the candy bar. With the candy bar it's calories.) Professor Owen Gingrich of Harvard figures that's "about fifty stars for every man, woman and child on earth."

And you thought you were poor! Not when you own fifty stars.

How much is that in terms of the long green? Look at it this way: If land is selling at $5,000 per acre in the New Jersey swamps, it must be worth twice that much on a nice, clean star where there are no mosquitos "and the skies are not cloudy all day." And how many acres in a star? A whole heck of a lot, I'd say; but be conservative, make it one acre per star. At ten thou per acre, that's half a million dollars in your pie in the sky. Not bad for someone who flunked beginner's astronomy.

Actually, it could probably be a whole lot more, because some of those stars are pretty big. But even at that low figure — wahoo! Your ship has come in, and it's a star-ship loaded with the big bucks. Thank you, Professor Gingrich, wherever you are.

Hello, IRS!

What are you going to do with your stars? Maybe you could sell one or two to a developer and go live your days in a condominium on the Gulf Coast, eating Godiva choclates all day and watching old *Star Trek* episodes on your Betamax, while the remainder of your stars just sit up there appreciating in value. They aren't making many new ones these days, and that always drives the price up. Maybe you could put a few of them out to the land bank and get paid for not doing anything with them. That could get you elected to Congress, you know.

It may trouble you that your stars are far away from you. You'd probably like to run your hand over a few of them just to make sure they're real. "A bird in the hand," as the saying goes. Astronomers like to talk in light-years and say things like, "The star you saw last night died a thousand years ago." Even Professor Gingrich says that some of ours could be dead already and we won't know it for another millennium. So, you'd just like to see a few of them on your bank account, just to be sure. That's understandable.

Of course, you must tithe your stars; that's the Christian way. It also confounds the IRS. They just hate it when people tithe. And think what it could do for the church. Ten per cent of fifty stars; that's five stars from each of us. And, say your church has 500 members. Presto! The church would have 2500 stars in its crown, or in its endowment fund, whichever comes first. You could pay off the mortgage. You could get a roof that doesn't leak. You could lay some carpet to muffle the sound of the lady elders' heels when they serve Communion. You could even have doughnuts with your Sunday morning coffee time. Talk about spiritual growth . . .!

But don't wait too long to get started. Your stars may not be ready to expire for a couple of eons, but as the Romans used to say, "Tempis fidgets." And besides, any tithe you get in before December thirty-first is deductible this year.

So, the next clear night, go outside and count your fifty to make sure they're all there. And then start that tithe. When the day star from on high cometh, you don't want to be found owing all those taxes.

Proverbs a la Carte

Some people in high places are saying we're going to restore our glorious American heritage by putting the Bible back in the schools. Maybe we ought to take a look at the role the Bible has played in our history. Consider the Book of Proverbs. Did you know that in colonial times Proverbs was the most popular book of the Bible? That's probably because it is one of the wisdom books, and our founding fathers were men of wisdom, like Benjamin Franklin, Thomas Jefferson, and the man who invented Friday.

My own list of favorites from Proverbs includes:

> *Three things are too wonderful for me;*
> *Four I do not understand:*
> > *the way of an eagle in the sky,*
> > *the way of a serpent on a rock,*
> > *the way of a ship on the high seas,*
> > *the way of a man with a maiden.*

Make that five:

> *the way of a waitress when you want more coffee.*

Another I like is:

> *Do not boast about tomorrow,*
> > *for you know not what a day may bring forth;*
> > *to say nothing of the five-day forecast.*

And there's:

> *Happy is the man who finds wisdom,*
> > *and the man who gets understanding,*
> *for the gain from it is better than silver,*
> > *and its profit better than gold:*
> *and they are not taxable until you are*
> > *three score years and ten.*

All through this marvelous book you'll find inspiration like that for your daily battle. Just close your eyes, let the book fall open, and the Holy Spirit will point your finger to your verse for the day. This morning he pointed mine to

> *A false balance is an abomination to the Lord,*
> *but a just weight is his delight.*

Well, I had just looked at my weight, and it was no delight. But there was the message: You can't hide from the Holy Spirit, even in your own bathroom.

This matter of how to let the Holy Spirit give you a message has produced some of Christianity's most ingenious practices. Not everyone takes the simple Ouija board approach. A woman I once knew always copied down the hymn numbers on Sunday and played them all week in the lottery. She believed that those numbers were planted in the preacher's head by the Spirit, and she didn't want to be guilty of denying the Spirit. "It's the unforgivable sin," she would respond to any questioner, "Matthew 12, point 32."

Some people think that the inspiring of Scripture was done at the factory, in the writing of the book itself. What bothers me about that approach is that I'm never sure which factory was the one where the Spirit worked. Was it the King James factory, the *Revised Standard Version* factory, the *Good News for Modern Man* factory, the *Scofield Chain Reference* (with the words of Jesus in red) factory? Only one of them can be the Spirit-inspired version, unless the Spirit is everywhere, like Santa Claus and Ronald McDonald.

Of course, that just may be the point. Not that the Spirit resembles Santa Claus or Ronald McDonald, but that she is everywhere. At least he is everywhere the Word is. Just open the book and there is instant charisma! The truth is, the Bible was charismatic long before people decided to be. Many an ancient believer reveled in such things as,

*For the lack of wood the fire goes out,
so why don't you switch to gas?*

and,

*Oil and perfume make the heart glad,
but they're no substitute for soap and water.*

Up, Up, a Little Bit Higher

Some people are saying that we ought to have an elevated choir. That's not the same as an *a cappella* choir, a Bach choir, or an *oratorio* choir. It isn't even like a concert choir or a touring choir. All it means is that you build a platform under them so they'll be up a little higher and can see the director better, and so their children can see if they behave any better during the sermon than they expect their children to do.

The choir doesn't have to do anything to get elevated. Some people have performed miracles in the church to be elevated to sainthood, but the only miracle the choir performs is showing up every week for rehearsal, in spite of viruses, babysitter problems, and husbands who have to fly to Atlanta or somewhere on two hours' notice.

You should understand that there's a difference between getting elevated and getting high. The choir may be high sometimes too, but it's because of some particularly well done rendition of something from Handel or Palestrina, not because of something they've inhaled. A choir on a Mozart high is a fearsome sight to behold, and if you've ever seen one soaring on the *capriccios* of Charles Ives, you know what "far out" means. But elevated is just raised up six inches by pine boards, nothing spiritual about it.

One of the things a wise old seminary mentor taught was "Never do anything always." He also once said, "Beware of Baptists bearing gifts." I never figured out that one, nor Baptists, to tell you the truth, but I've always heeded his advice to "treat your choir well, because the choir can be the war department of the church." A war we can do without. So, maybe we weren't exactly paying the piper when we bought them new robes and built them a new closet, but you'll notice that they haven't been threatening recently to sing the entire Fauré Requiem for an offertory, in Latin.

The danger in elevating the choir may be that you'll set other departments to thinking about "perks." Suppose the Sunday church school teachers start asking for merit pay for showing up on time. What if committee chairmen demand expense accounts and an 800 number to the church? Or Session members want access to the executive washroom and the pastor's Godiva chocolate supply? I don't know where you would draw your line, but you've just crossed mine.

Why should everyone want to be elevated anyway? Sometimes the best things aren't *up*. Great men don't go *up* in history. Stephen C. Foster didn't long for "Way *Up* Upon the Suwannee River." Heaven may not be *up*, either. The Lord's Prayer doesn't say it's up or down or even out, although once Jesus said it is "within you," which could mean up one day and down the next. Personally, I've always thought of heaven as down, like down in the Caribbean in February. A man's heaven is where his heart is, which reminds me of the clergy-person who said he wouldn't go to heaven until they got a decent eighteen-hole golf course. "Good news," said his friend. "They've just opened one, and your tee off time is tomorrow morning at seven."

Jesus said the way to get elevated is to take the lowest seat at a banquet and perhaps the master of the house will bid you come up higher. I've always gotten a rise out of that. On the other hand, your host might ignore you like he never saw you before and leave you miserably unelevated and mumbling in your snapper soup. Not to worry, luv. In the Father's house are many rooms and they are all on the top floor, even for the likes of you and me and the choir.

Senior Citizen Discount

There's a trend developing in our country that I don't like the looks of at all. I mean the way they're starting to take "senior citizen" to mean sixty, and even fifty-five. It's like they can't wait to get at us. Time was when you had to be old enough for Medicare before you could get special treatment on trains and the like, and we all agreed that it was right to give old-timers a break. The first time I saw "discount for senior citizens sixty or over," I shrugged it off and said, "If anybody's that hard up to save a quarter, let him have it." But when one of my favorite eateries began offering the senior citizen specials to fifty-five-year olds, I threw in my napkin and said, "You've gone too far, Guiseppe." I can't enjoy eating in any place where they call fifty-five "senior." Which is a shame, because they served a terrific lasagna. But a person has to draw a line and stand by it, whatever the sacrifice. "Man doesn't live by lasagna alone," the Good Book says, "for life is more than meat and drink."

Now that I've cleverly got the Bible on my side, I can proceed with truly righteous indignation, which is the best kind, and by far the most fun.

It's not that I think being "senior" is bad. Some of my best friends are seniors, and I would have them in my home anytime and trust them a lot more than some of our own kind. Maybe I wouldn't want my daughter to marry one of them, but I'm not against them. And I'm not saying that being young is really any better. When I was "youth" I didn't find it all free and easy. I had all the appetites but very little of the wherewithal; now I haven't so many appetites and still not much of the wherewithal. But it's at least a fair compromise. As one of our legislators said of a recent law restoring the death penalty, "It's an arrangement we can live with."

What I don't like is this subtle raiding of my "middle-age" sanctuary. I mean, I've been a middle-ager too many years to change now. I like it here. It's comfortable. I know where everything is, what to expect, and how to get out of the worst jobs. When the time comes to move on I'll go like all the rest and take my pension check, Geritol, and shuffleboard with good grace. But don't be making plans for me just because I've celebrated "the big 6-oh." Wait till I have my first Social Security check in hand before you tell me I'm a senior. Until then, it's middle age all the way, Pierre.

Where's the Bible in all this? Well, the Bible sure doesn't say, "Grow old along with me, the best is yet to be." That was Robert Browning, and just look where he is now. The Bible doesn't talk about growing old so much as about growing *up*, like in "When I became a man I put away childish things," and like not believing in the Bible. (That's from 1 Corinthians 13, in case you haven't grown up enough to start believing in the Bible.) It tells about people who were man enough — okay, or woman enough — to stand up with Jesus and believe that the world is hopeless without him. The only real senior citizen it said much about was Methuselah, and the gist of it was that he lived 969 years without doing anything worthwhile. That may take some planning, but it's hardly commendable. Even misspent youth and wasted manhood are not as bad as growing old useless, then growing older useless, and finally growing oldest, still useless. God wants something of us for his investment.

The whole trouble for me in all of this is that I really don't know any old people. Senior citizens, yes. Golden agers, sure. Respected elders, you bet. But they're all so young, and I'm not far behind them, and neither are you, my friend. Still, for now I'll pay full price for my lasagna, Antoine. Somehow it tastes better that way.

The Nicest Words

When a couple of newspaper columnists asked their readers to vote on a list of the ten most beautiful words in the English language, they ended with a tie between "melody" and "velvet" for the top spot. There was also a tie for third place between "gossamer" and "crystal." None of those words would have topped my list. I have always found surpassing pleasure in the word "mozzarella," said with a long, loving hold on the ls.

In fact, for a person of Irish ancestry, I have an unusual fondness for the music of any well-spoken Italian words. What can beat *bella bella*, or *fettuccini*, or *parmesan*, pronounced "parma jonna" with the third syllable accented? The fact that they all have to do with gustatorial delight is incidental, but not accidental, and reminds me of my intense dislike for any "dental," whether acci-, inci-, or just plain. I don't like "gustatorial," either. It suggests "shoveling it in," which is no way to enjoy good food. I suppose that what this leads to is a list that has the ten most ugly words with beautiful meanings, like "purple," *regnum*, and "eleemosynary."

The list of ten most beautiful words included no names, but I would certainly vote for Mary, a name which has both beauty of sound and of biblical association. I would include Laura for a favorite niece, a lovely song, and its own mellowness. My all-time favorite name belonged to a former president of the Soviet Union, Nicolai Podgorny. When you give a slight Slovak touch to the middle syllable of the first name and role the "r" in Podgorny, you have a name that you can just go around all day enjoying. I used to say Nicolai Podgorrrny every time I got the blahs. It gave me a lift the way seeing a vase of flowers on a rainy day will do, or smelling the apples I have stored in the basement refrigerator. Excuse me while I say it again . . . Nicolai Podgorrrny. Ah, that felt good.

The Irish, the Old Irish, that is, have the word *mulcahy*.

It's their equivalent to the English "bloke" and the American "guy." But "bloke" and "guy" have none of the sensual quality of *mulcahy* said in the true Irish way. There's a bit of a taste to it, like the taste of a fresh Irish potato, kind of earthy and a little wild. Try it with the accent on the second syllable and the "a" sounding as it does in "cat."

Most of the beauty in biblical words comes from their meaning, not from their sound. "Grace" identifies probably the most beautiful concept in the entire history of human thought, but as a sound it has nothing special to it. Maybe what that tells us is to look to the inner reality, not the outer sensuality. *Elohim*, *El Shaddai*, and *Adonai*, all biblical names for God, seem to me to have little in their sound to commend them (for that matter "God" isn't a particularly melodic sound), but the reality which those names represent makes them words of supreme value to us.

The reason biblical words aren't much for beauty of sound is that they originate in ancient Hebrew, Greek, or Aramaic, none of them soft and melodious the way Italian is, for example. Yet, there are exceptions. In the story about the healing of Jairus' little daughter, Jesus calls the child by a loving Aramaic name, *talitha*, "little girl." I'm always pleasured by that delightful word. Doesn't it sound just like your little granddaughter? Go ahead, be my guest, say a couple of *talitha's* for yourself right now . . . There, wasn't that nice?

I'm not sure whether we could make a list of the ten most beautiful church words. "Transcept," "antependium," "reredos," "covered-dish," all have much holiness of tradition to them, but they aren't cherished for their sound. "Ay-men" and "ah-men," even "alleluia" and "hallelujah" go a long way back with us, but they don't compare in melody with "mozzarella," *mulcahy*, or "Nicolai Podgorrrny." Neither does "finally," but there's no word in all of the church's lexicon that can make people sigh with pure delight like a good "finally" in a sermon when the preacher really means it.

Beauty may be, after all, in the eye, or in this case the ear, of the beholder — or behearer. So it is with the name "Jesus." If you don't know the man behind the name, the sound of it won't warm your heart. It's a bit shrill, to tell the truth. But as John Newton's hymn so rightly puts it,

> *How sweet the name of Jesus sounds,*
> *in a believer's ear!*
> *It soothes his sorrow, heals his wounds,*
> *and drives away his fear.*

It's more beautiful even than "mozzarella."

Preacher in the Pew

People tell me that I should go visit other churches on my vacation Sundays. "Get some fresh ideas," they say. "See what it's like down in the pews. The change will do you good."
I'm touched.
Of course, I have always gone to church on vacation, and over the years I've learned a few lasting lessons. One is that pews are hard in anybody's theology — Baptist, Lutheran, Reformed, or even Free Spirit. One of the longest sermons I ever heard was on liberation theology. The preacher liberated our spirits in no time, but he kept our bodies in captivity for well over an hour until the dead-end syndrome was rampant. Even with pew cushions and plenty of natural padding on the worshiper, a mere twenty-five minute sermon reaches the numbness threshold about a third of the way along. That's when you begin to see heads appear here and there across the congregation as people rise off their seats an inch or two to restore circulation. Jesus knew about the dead-end syndrome, which is why even his famous Sermon on the Mount was only about ten or twelve minutes long. The people all said that "he spoke as one having authority," but he also spoke as one who knew about dead ends. Those people were sitting out there on rocks!
I don't get as much conditioning to pew sitting as laymen do, which is probably why my numbness threshold is very low. I go dead before the preacher even gets to "And secondly . . ." Some Presbyterians who wind up in a Lutheran church on vacation complain about all the getting up and down, but personally I appreciate any service that gives me a chance to get the blood flowing again.
Another lasting lesson from church visiting is that you can never hide the fact that you are a clergyman. Maybe it's the way we usually sit down front, just to prove a point. Maybe it's the way we take notes. It could be the shameless way we sing hymns

as though they were meant to be heard. I've gone to church in a sport shirt and pastel slacks and had people say to me, "You don't look like a minister, but you sure do sing like one."

There are good reasons for trying to hide your divinity when you are in another man's vineyard. One is that he might call you up to do the benediction, or offer a prayer, or, heaven forbid, ask you to say a few words. "Just whatever the Spirit gives unto thee." Usually I'm asking the Spirit to give unto me some relief from my numbness. Another reason to conceal your "reverendity" is so the poor preacher won't get nervous about having another cleric in the congregation who might recognize some stories from last month's *Preacher's Digest*.

Even if you stay anonymous right to the end, there's a good chance you'll give yourself away at the door. It's probably the way you shake hands and say, "I like the way you handled the second part of that text." You can just see the "uh-oh" on his face. He's also a bit let down, because he thought you were from a pulpit committee.

Once we were in a place where there was simply no church anywhere. That's not the lucky break you might think. It was, in fact, a most depressing day. And that's where I learned my most lasting lesson, which is that a permanent vacation may be heaven, but if you can never find a church — it's hell.

Holy Ingenuity

After six years and three major repair jobs, the Property Committee still had trouble with a leak that dripped from the ceiling in the Sunday church school closet. "What you've got there is your classic beam runner," the man from the roofing company informed them. "The water comes in on one of the beams and runs along it who knows how far till it finds an outlet. A lot of your old churches have them."

With that bit of news, he zipped up his jacket and headed for his truck. As far as he was concerned, a problem named is a problem solved.

As far as the insurance company was concerned, it was an act of God, "and we don't cover that," said the agent. "I guess that's your department, isn't it, Reverend?" he concluded with a snicker.

So "Reverend" took care of it. He got a bucket and put it under the drip and instructed the sexton to empty it every Saturday, or when it was full, whichever came first. And that was that — $36,000 for the roof, and the floor stays dry because of a two-dollar bucket. *Quod perficit, perficit* (what works, works).

The Property Committee decided to make a survey of the whole church to see what other repairs were needed. They found that "the Reverend" had used his brand of fix-it in a lot of places, and all that the new Five-Year Plan for Preventive Maintenance needed to do was replace a few worn-out parts.

For instance, the main entrance from the parking lot is a double door equipped with an automatic plunger device, panic bars, safety glass, and a broom handle that holds it open in hot weather. The committee found a crack in the broom handle, so they bought the sexton a new broom, cut the handle from his old one for the door, and sawed the cracked one into wedges to hold up the windows in the social hall that keep sliding down.

What the committee was discovering, of course, was something every practicing pastor knows about from day one — Holy Ingenuity. It's one of the great unrecognized virtues of the faith. You may not see it in theology books, or on architectural drawings, but if you go through any church and look in back of things and around behind corners and beneath ledges, you'll see a whole other ecclesiastical world where Holy Ingenuity is the true Saving Grace. And if you go into the pastor's study and look on the shelf nearest his desk, you'll see his copy of the classic volume, *The Role of Paper Clips, Tape and Rubber Bands in the Reformed Faith*, more commonly known as Calvin's Substitutes.

Search committees should realize that a strong sense of Holy Ingenuity can be as valuable in a minister as charisma, sound theology, or good looks. Take the case of the crack in the Transfiguration of Our Lord Memorial Stained Glass Window. One member said that she could see daylight right through Peter's left foot. Well, the man from the art glass studio came out and examined it and said that it could be taken care of, but it would mean replacing the entire lower left panel all the way up to Peter's knees and part of John's *gluteus maximus*. "You can't just cut across glass like this with a pair of scissors, you know," he declared. Then he quoted a price.

"*Id obliviscetur!*" ("Forget it!") said "the Reverend." The next day he went in and fixed the crack his own way. You can't really tell that there was ever a crack there, and you have to get your nose up real close to Peter's foot before you can smell the faint scent of bubble gum. It not only saved the church a lot of money, but also saved John's *gluteus maximus*.

I know that in our congregation we couldn't survive without H.I., as we call it at property meeting. You take our pipe organ, for example. It's the most expensive thing we have in the church, except the minister, but it's our pride and joy. The craftsmanship is exquisite, and it's bigger than the one the Lutherans have. If you look closely at the hand-carved music rack on the console, you'll see two bright red rubber bands wrapped around it to hold the organist's hymnbook open. Our service contract calls for the organ people to come once a month and tune the instrument, clean the contacts, and replace the rubber bands. You don't spare costs when it comes to a valuable pipe organ.

I don't mean to say that only ministers and musicians can use Holy Ingenuity. I know better from personal experience. A few summers back the church dipped into the Memorial Fund to buy an air conditioner for the office. They didn't just get one from Cheap John's either. They called in an air conditioning engineer, and he recommended one that offered super quiet and complete climate control. It was worth the cost. That first summer the staff worked in blessed comfort, and the bulletins came out sharp, clean, and crisp. But when winter came, cold air poured in underneath the air conditioner. Three visits from the air conditioning engineer didn't help, but the problem was solved when the secretary went across the hall to the ladies' room and got paper towels and stuffed them into the crack. Now all we have to do is replace the paper towels each October and we've got climate control year-round.

It's the same all across this land of the free and home of the brave. From the little white frame churches of New England to the alabaster cathedrals of California, the observant churchgoer will discover pulpit lamps with cardboard extensions fastened to them to keep the light from glaring in the preacher's glasses, the Apostles' Creed taped to lecterns in case of mental blank, thumb tacks holding antependia in place, old bulletins wedged under wobbly-footed Communion tables, and matchsticks jammed into amplifier controls to keep anyone from turning up the P.A. system too far. As the Scriptures say, "He who has eyes to see, let him see."

And while he's at it, let him see all the human rubber bands and paper clips that hold the church together and make it work. They're God's bits of Holy Ingenuity.

Balconies

Some churches have balconies and some do not. I'm glad ours doesn't, for a balcony can be a dangerous place. I remember a church in my home town that was supposed to have a haunted balcony. The legend was that an old man had gone up into the balcony and hung himself. Ever after that his ghost drifted around up there, and sometimes you could hear him moaning and sighing, especially at night after prayer meeting. This gave the people an excuse for avoiding prayer meeting.

My own fear of balconies began when our Sunday church school teacher showed us a picture of Samson's destruction of the Philistines. There was Samson, standing in the temple, pushing against the pillars with all his terrible might. And the pillars collapsed, and down came the roof and the balcony of the temple. The picture showed vividly the terror on the faces of the people as they plunged to their deaths from the collapsing balcony. I've been afraid of balconies ever since. Also of giants with long hair.

Some balconies in American churches were built originally as places for the slaves, who should worship but not too close to their white masters. (Well, you know, it might rub off.) They admitted what Paul had written about "neither slave nor free," but they quickly pointed out that he didn't say anything about sitting together. Nowadays those balconies are a special haven for people who like to come late and leave early and don't care to get involved in the singing. You can slip unnoticed into the balcony and just sit up there, closer to heaven, and look down on the people below, and be first out at the end. Sometimes the ushers even forget to come up there during the offering. Some folks won't go to a church that doesn't have a balcony.

Actually, it is incorrect to say that our church has no balcony, because every church has a spiritual balcony. In fact, the spiritual balcony in many churches is the biggest part of the church. Sometimes half the membership is up there. The danger isn't from overcrowding, however, and certainly not from modern giants gone berserk. In fact, it's really a very safe place to be. That's the danger! That, plus the likelihood that "when the role is called up yonder," the people in the balcony will be only on stand-by.

Prayerfully Consider

A church that urges its families "to prayerfully consider" can't be all bad. You may rightly wince at this splitting of infinitives in the House of the Lord, but you can't deny that something "prayerfully considered" seems a whole lot more Christian than something just "considered." You can't fault a church for trying to add a little sanctity to its appeal (or a little appeal to its sanctity, which also is sometimes sorely needed).

As for splitting infinitives in church, the end justifies the means. "Have you never read what David did when he was an hungered, and all with him: how he entered the House of God and did eat the shewbread which it was not lawful for him to eat" (Mark 2:25), for goodness sake? Is splitting an unsanctified infinitive any worse than cleaving a holy loaf? Like the sabbath, the grammar was made for man, not man for the grammar. If David could "eat the shewbread," we can split an infinitive here and there when it's in the Lord's cause.

My dis-ease is not with the looseness of epistolatory grammar, but with the possible gratuitousness of its strategy. (And there's a mouthful.) That is to say, what exactly do we think the prayerful considerers will do that will differ from the non-prayerful? Will the prayerful use holier words, like "thou," "thee" and "thine," "shalt," "wilt," and "art"? In prayerful considering, does the considering comes first and then the praying, or the praying first and then the considering? Or will one person do the considering, like Dad with the budget book open, and another do the praying, like Mom with the Bible open?

Dad: Well, that's it. I've considered it, and we can afford one dollar a month.

Mom: Wait, we have "to prayerfully consider."

Dad: Oh! . . . Well, let us pray, "O Lord, a, um . . . we, ah, think we should give sacrificially . . . ah, like, ah, say, one dollar a month. In Jesus name. Amen.

Now there's a family that's going to go down to the mall feeling much better for having prayerfully considered. It leaves the conscience wonderfully clear.

Nothing is without risk, though. One family was prayerfully considering their one dollar a week decision when they got a bit too prayerful and actually heard God's reply:

"Make it $5 a week, on account of inflation," he saith unto them.

I mean, when you decide "to prayerfully consider," you'd better be prepared to succeed now and then. That family not only split the infinitive with the Lord, they also split the difference with him and made it two-fifty per week.

I asked my friend over at the Church of the Free Spirit if they ever considered prayerfully considering. "Once," he replied, "but it didn't work. I had asked all our families 'to prayerfully consider' going out as missionaries for a year. I got only one reply. It said, 'A family that prays together stays together, and this family's staying right here.' They also asked if I had 'prayerfully considered' going myself."

Ministers themselves do prayerfully consider things. For instance, they do it when an offer comes from another church. They take all the facts and figures and retire to the study "to prayerfully consider" the call. And it always works. If it's a small church, the answer always comes out "no." If it's a larger church, the answer always comes back "yes." Women's intuition is sometimes way ahead of men's prayerful considering. While he's in there talking it over with the Lord, she already knows from the size of the offer whether she should start packing or just get on with supper.

I'll tell you one thing, though. What I prayerfully consider the most is that the Lord remembers "to prayerfully consider" when he's looking at my record and deciding what to do with me. I figure my chances are much better if he's praying about it.

The More Things Change

Jesus Christ may be the same yesterday, today, and forever, but you can hardly be that sure of who anybody else really is. Take the other Sunday afternoon when I went to a concert — not my usual way to spend a Sunday afternoon. I tend more toward sleeping on the sofa with the football game on the TV. Anyway, on the program that afternoon was a pair of interpretative dancers — not my usual preference on a concert program. I lean toward brass quartets that aren't afraid to play recognizable tunes. Nonetheless, these two girls were pretty good, and also very shapely and sensuous in their black leotards. Their names were Fred and Roger! I mean, you never know, do you?

Of course, it's anybody's right not to be what we think he is, or she is, or even it is. For one thing, people change. I ran into an old third grade pal the other day and almost didn't recognize him. He was digging lustily into a huge leafy salad loaded with radishes and raw carrots and the like. If it hadn't been for the wart on his nose, I never would have believed that he was the sniffy little runt I used to know who would rather have taken a bath or a piano lesson than touch a salad. Now he sports a bumper sticker that says, "This car stops at all salad bars." Time changes all of us. In this case, it was helped by his wife who said, "Shape up or ship out . . ."

Even I have not always been what you see now. You may think that I have had this halo since day one, but the truth is I started out with a pair of horns. At the age of six I had already flunked Junior Church three times, and when I was a teenager I published a list of "Ten Ways to be Sick at Sunday Church School Time and Miraculously Recovered for Lunch." I was the only kid in the church to be offered to the Baptists for a future draft choice and an old pair of waders. I was no bargain to the Lord. The halo didn't show up till much later. If you think it still hasn't, you have to look when the light hits it from the proper angle. Otherwise it's there but invisible . . . really.

It can be disconcerting not to be sure of things anymore. An apple a day used to keep the doctor away, but now it's the sales quota for a computer company. A penny saved may still be a penny earned, but it's no longer worth a red cent, a plug nickel, nor even a thin dime. Even a dollar hardly pays for the wear and tear on the offering plate, which you might keep in mind next Sunday.

All this duplicity can make for problems in the church. What red-blooded minister has not greeted someone he thought was a stranger only to discover that it was a charter member who had got a new hair style and contacts? What well-meaning dozer in the pew has not roused himself and begun gathering his things for a quick departure because he thought "and in conclusion" meant that the sermon was about to end? Things are not what they seem, and my advice to you is that you should look at least twice before you leap into any conclusions. It could be a tub of hot water.

It's gotten so bad that even sin is affected. You can't be sure anymore whether a thing is sin or just sophistication. Time was when the really big sins were things like drinking, gambling, and staying out all night. Now that's called "macho," and sin is being overweight and having psoriasis. It's hard to know whether you ought to read the Ten Commandments or the Pritikin Diet book.

All is not lost, though. I'm still me, and you're still you, and the twain of us still meet at eleven on Sunday with the Lord in the midst of us. When we can no longer count on that, it really is time to start worrying.

I'd Like to Know

There's a legend — if there isn't, I'll start one — that every newcomer to heaven gets a five-minute audience with the Lord as a gesture of welcome. If you think you're going to make it, I suggest you sit down now and decide what you're going to talk about, so you don't waste your time allotment on "Hello, how're you doin'? What do you think of this weather we've been having lately?"

I plan to use my time to find out some things I've always wanted to know but didn't know whom to ask. Like, how come whenever you get jelly in a restaurant it's always grape? I mean, that's a serious matter. Did someone make grape our national fruit? Where is there a law that you shouldn't put a little strawberry in there sometimes? or maybe even a little orange marmalade? Lord knows, I hope.

And how come when you order coffee they bring you nice brewed coffee in a steaming glass pot, but when you ask for decaffeinated you get a cup of warm water and a little envelope with some brown powder that when you dump it into the water looks like something you'd dye an Easter egg in? And if you want another cup it's another forty cents. Where did it say on the tablets Moses brought down from the mountain that you shouldn't make decaf in a pot?

And where is it carved in stone that every electrical outlet in the house has to be behind something? And that T-shirts always have to shrink? And that zippers only jam when you're in a hurry?

These are important questions in humanity's search for eternal meaning, and I plan to ask them. I'm not going to waste my five minutes on trivial things like how did Adam have the time and energy to sin for us all. Or is the millenium going to be pre-, post-, or whatever? I want the real secrets of the universe. Like, how do you get a cereal box open without ripping the lid all apart. How do you find what happened to the pencil you put by the telephone when everyone says, "Don't ask me, I didn't touch it." Where do shut-ins go when you call on them and they aren't at home? Why are the back pews more comfortable than the front ones? I'm dying to know, literally.

I don't know how many questions can be asked in five minutes. I recall something about one day in His sight being like a thousand years (that's 2 Peter 3:9). That computes out to be a mighty long five minutes, and even I haven't that many complaints; and I doubt that He has that much patience. But I do need to know things like why our holiest days always come on Easter and Christmas when the schools are closed and everyone's gone away. (My friend at the Church of the Free Spirit says that over there they don't announce them in advance, they just wait for a Sunday when there's a full house, and then they have Christmas or Easter.) And I want to know why we couldn't have had two Saturdays in every weekend. Then maybe some of my members could have got all yard work and shopping and golf games done and been able to get to church when Sunday finally did come. I think there was just a bit of poor planning there, and I intend to say so. It might be my only opportunity before I get transferred.

The Cookie Monster

One of my greatest fears is that the world will run out of cookies. I dream it at night and wake up weeping, but I fear that one of these times it will be real. Against that day of Armageddon I keep a supply of Lorna Doones hidden away, but in my heart of hearts I know that they wouldn't last long in a real crisis. Oh, who will deliver me from the dark dread, this fearsome cookiephobia? That ancient Latin, Virgil, said, "*Deceneres anomos timor arguit*," (look it up). But what did he know about chocolate chips, brownies, or peanut butter divinities?

There, I've bared my misery to you. Now, will you confess? What's your greatest fear? Write it on a box of Pecan Sandies and send it to me. It will do you good to get it off your chest, and out of your house.

And don't worry that you are the only one. I know lots of Christians who live in dread of being caught in an offering with only a twenty dollar bill in their pockets. And look how many are terrified of sitting too far from the door in case of earthquake. There are even those who are apprehensive lest the person in front of them should turn around and catch them singing the hymn, or worse, enjoying the sermon. Being a Christian has its hazards, some even worse than lions in arenas.

Fear can make people do terrible things. My own personal dread, for instance, has led me more than once to go on the cookie wagon. Now isn't that a shameful humiliation for a proud man to bear? Just try forcing yourself to request longer sermons, if you want to know how painful it can be. I've seen agony in the faces of people who gave up their back pews for Lent. I've witnessed the torment of a man forcing himself to confess that he liked one of the hymns I picked. I've literally felt the quaking of church members trying to overcome their dread of committees. It's no easy thing to face down your fear, but there's no true peace for one who is forever running away from dragons. As that ancient Greek, Sophocles, said, "*Ei qui timet omnia crepitant.*" (Figure it out.)

The thing about fears is that they are seldom well-founded. Most of what we dread never really happens. I mean, the world can't really run out of cookies, can it? As long as there are church meetings there will be cookies. In fact, as long as there are any kind of meetings, there will be cookies. I've had some of my best binges at the social hour after a PTA meeting. I don't know what atheists have to meet about, but if they do, I'm sure they have cookies, probably devil's food, or those meringues that are empty inside. To each his own, you know.

So try to reason with your fears. Tell yourself that we don't really have unscheduled offerings or Sunday earthquakes, and that that man in front of you is too worried that you will catch him singing to turn around and catch you. And who's to know that you actually listen to the sermons, if you don't tell them? Your fears are all in your head. Put them away and come to church with a clear conscience and an open mind. As that great Democrat Franklin D. Roosevelt said, "*Solo res quae nobis timendum est timor ipse est.*" (Guess.)

Start Praying

With Lent coming up, a lot of people will be wanting to pray, but they'll hesitate because they don't know the right words. They get as far as "Heavenly Father" and then they draw a blank. If that's your problem, I can have you praying like a trooper quicker than you can say "Second Helvetic Confession." It's all done with a Bible.

Let's say you're on your way to a dental appointment. I don't know of a better time for a lesson or prayer. Open your Bible and look at Psalm 1.

Blessed is the man who walketh not with a mouth full of cavities,
  nor standeth in the need of drilling,
  nor sitteth in the seat of the oral surgeon;
But his delight is in teeth that are plastic,
  and with his dentures he smileth night and day.

Okay? You're off to a good start. Now let's try a public prayer. Say you've been asked to give the invocation at the local Republican Club fundraiser. Try Psalm 136.

O give thanks to the President, for he is good;
  His tax cuts endureth forever.

You're doing just fine. You've already learned two prayers in less than five minutes. Stick with Psalm 136 and you can make it three in six minutes, or even four in seven. Like this:

O give thanks for the new dishwasher, for it is good;
  It destroyeth the Tupperware forever.

O give thanks to the neighbor's new dog, for he is good;
  He chaseth away cats forever.

O give thanks for the cable TV, for it is good;
  It re-runneth McHale's Navy forever.

Enough of 136. Your prayers could get in a rut. Let's try the New Testament. Paul had some great prayers we could use. I've always liked his 1 Corinthians 13 for letting it all hang out.

And now abideth lettuce, celery and chocolate, these three;
But the greatest of these is chocolate.

Now we know what Paul's "thorn-in-the-flesh" was. He was a closet chocoholic. Makes the rest of us sinners feel better already. Of course, you can add your own last line, "But the greatest of these is cheesecake . . . pate de fois gra . . . the Whopper" . . . Whatever your passion may be.

The main thing is to tell it all to the Lord. Remember, "what peace we often forfeit, all because we do not." So, happy prayers, and meanwhile I'll see if I can get your favorite indulgence taken off the sin list for the holidays.

The Future Is in the Bag

Not everyone was too busy with other things to miss the 100th anniversary of the paper bag. Yet, even as we celebrated, there was a cloud on the sack scene. It's plastic, as in plastic bags, thin and slick, with hand holes cut in them and snappy logos printed on their sides. The plastic sack is threatening to send the paper bag to its "just reward," as the theology bunch would say. The sack is in danger of being sacked.

"We're concerned," admits Davis H. Carelton, head of the (honest-to-goodness) "brown paper bag division" of the American Paper Institute. "Concerned, but not panicked." Which is exactly what Pharaoh said when he saw all the frogs and gnats, and the Nile River turning to blood: "Concerned, but not panicked." Better he should have panicked. (Better for him, not for us. We like the way it turned out.)

I'm not sure I like the way the bag situation threatens to turn out, though. Let's face it, we've learned to love these faithful servants. They carry out our garbage, keep our galoshes from mildewing during the summer, and even serve as luggage when all the suitcases are full. And how do you think we carry all the money to the bank on Sunday afternoon? The threatened demise of the paper bag is not a happy thought for those of us who appreciate simple utility. It is downright traumatic for people who remember the smell of a Maine lobster, fresh and pink from the cook pot, carried home in a paper bag; or the aroma of a sack full of cinnamon buns still warm from the baker's oven. What plastic ever smelled like anything but plastic?

Maybe if the paper bag had been invented sooner it would have earned tenure, and then you couldn't replace it even if you did invent something better. And who's to say that it wouldn't have been useful to our forefathers. King James might have carried his first Version in one of them. Martin Luther could have carried his hammer and nails and ninety-five theses in one.

He might even have had room for the other five arguments he left at home. And don't ask me what they were. I don't even know any of the first ninety-five. Go ask a Lutheran. He probably won't know either, but he will be certain that they were right, whatever they were. And after all, do you know all the chapters in the Westminster Confession of Faith? And please don't say, "What's that?"

Anyway, it's the little things that count, and compared to the wheel, the lever, and the pasta machine, a paper bag might seem a very little thing indeed. Yet — I happen to know that Billy Graham stores his old sermons in a brown bag in the basement of Yankee Stadium. Norman Vincent Peale collects his positive thoughts in the same brown bag he started with in 1945. The Pope carries his sandwich in a brown bag when he goes to meet with the College of Cardinals. He calls it his brown Papal bag; the Cardinals call it the Pope-poke. And it was in a plain, unmarked paper bag that Madalyn Murray O'Hair smuggled her first prayers out of a classroom.

So, let's always remember that for those who have faith, the future is in the bag.

www.ingramcontent.com/pod-product-compliance
Lightning Source LLC
Chambersburg PA
CBHW060851050426
42453CB00008B/928